Table of Contents

We dedicate this book to you,

the entrepreneur, business owner, sales professional or consultant,
whether you are experienced or are just getting started.
You recognize the power of knowing what to do and when
to do it in order to have a wildly successful business.
We salute you for embracing more knowledge to advance
your business—and we celebrate your commitment
to being the best you can be!

The Co-Authors of *Incredible Business*

Acknowledgements

Gratitude is an important part of business success. Before we share our wisdom and experience with you, we have a few people to thank for turning our vision for this book into a reality.

This book is the brilliant concept of Caterina Rando, the founder of Thrive Publishing™ and a respected business speaker and strategist. Working closely with many of us over the years, Caterina realized how much value we have to share, and how much people could benefit from that knowledge. The result was putting our ideas into a comprehensive book. Without Caterina's "take action" spirit, her positive attitude and her commitment to excellence, you would not be reading this book, of which we are all so proud.

Additionally, all of our efforts were supported by a truly dedicated team who worked diligently to put together the best possible book for you. We are grateful for everyone's stellar contribution.

To Patricia Haddock, whose experience in copywriting and copyediting proved invaluable, and whose magic pen and expertise ensured that this book would be the best it could be.

To Ruth Schwartz, with her many years of experience and wisdom, who served as an ongoing guide throughout the project, your support to our production team and to all of the co-authors is deeply appreciated.

To Tammy Tribble and Tricia Principe, our designers extraordinaire, who brought their creative talents to the cover and book layout, thank you both for your enthusiasm, problem solving and attention to detail throughout this project.

To our exceptional proofreaders, Karen Gargiulo and Bernie Burson, thank you for ensuring we dotted all the i's, crossed all the t's and placed every comma where it belongs.

We also acknowledge each other for delivering outstanding information, guidance and advice to you. Through our work in this book and with our clients, we are truly committed to enhancing the success of business people throughout the world. We are truly grateful that we get to do work that we love, and contribute to so many in the process. We do not take our good fortune lightly. We are clear in our mission—to make a genuine contribution to you, the reader. Thank you for granting us this extraordinary opportunity.

The Co-Authors of *Incredible Business*

Introduction

Congratulations! You have opened an incredible resource, packed with great ideas that will enhance your business in ways you cannot yet imagine. You are about to discover how to build an incredible business.

Your business success comes as the result of more than talent, commitment and hard work. Your success will also be determined by the impression you make on current and prospective clients, how productively and effectively you run your business, and how well you communicate and create stellar customer service that keeps people returning to your business.

We know you want to be the absolute best you can be. With this book, you will quickly learn how successful business people get the very best results. As top experts in each of our respective specialties, we have joined to give you the most powerful information and strategies available.

Each of us has seen how even small changes can transform and uplift your business.

• Knowing how to use social networking sites to make key connections can increase your ability to grow your business, reach new markets and expand your customer base.

- Understanding how to focus your resources on tasks that have the greatest payback can improve your bottom line and reduce stress.

- Managing the mental side of business can help you take better care of your business and your life.

- And much more.

All the business professionals you will meet in this book want your business to succeed. We have outlined for you our top tips and included the most expert advice we have to advance your success.

To get the most out of *Incredible Business,* we recommend you read it once, cover to cover, then go back and follow the advice that applies to you, in the chapters most relevant to your current situation. Every improvement you make will increase your confidence and effectiveness and positively affect how others respond to your business.

Learning what to do will not create transformation. You must take action and apply the strategies, tips and tactics we share in these pages. Apply the many skills in this book, and you will reap many rewards. With our knowledge and your action, we are confident that, like our thousands of satisfied clients, you too will master the magic of how to conjure up an *Incredible Business.*

To your unlimited success!

The Co-Authors of *Incredible Business*

Getting through the Maze
of Starting a Business
By Sylvia A. Stern

"If you don't know where you're going
you'll probably end up somewhere else."
—David Campbell, Ph.D.,
Senior fellow, Center for Creative Leadership

I was walking down the aisle of a drugstore one day when I heard someone call my name.

He said, "Do you remember me? I used to work at IBM®. Are you still in business for yourself?"

I responded, "Yes."

He said, "Darn! What is your secret? I don't know how you did it; I tried it for a year and failed miserably."

After listening to his story, I realized that he had not figured out how to make it through this maze called "business." He did not have what I call "maze brightness." Maze brightness is being intelligent about the sometimes-confusing network of winding pathways in business.

To succeed in today's crazy business world, you must have the key to the maze. He had jumped right into starting a business without doing enough preparation. Going into business for yourself is much more than just saying, "I am going into business for myself."

Before leaving corporate America and starting my own business, I interviewed countless successful entrepreneurs who were in the consulting business, as I hoped to be. I heard about their colossal successes and their massive failures. They helped me develop maze brightness. Their valuable words and my 16 years in corporate America gave me a good understanding that it was not going to be easy, and if I did not plan and strategize, I could be out of business in a year.

I want to share what has helped me navigate through the confusing maze and into maze brightness. It has allowed me to stay in business for 17 years.

Acquiring Maze Brightness

Starting your own business is exciting and fun. I want you to succeed. I want you to stay in business—let me help you acquire some maze brightness.

First, you need to answer some important questions:

• Why do I want to own a business?

• What do I expect to accomplish?

• Does my product or service fulfill a need?

• Am I willing to work an 80- to 100-hour week?

• Do I have sufficient operating funds?

Still willing to go forward? Great. Let's get started.

Step One: Do Your Homework

After you have asked and answered these questions and are willing to go forward, then the first thing you need to do is to select ten to fifteen people who own businesses similar to your area of expertise. Call them and set up an appointment. Be prepared to pick their brains. Prepare a set of no more than five questions related to their expertise and ask each person the same questions. Be clear on what you want from them. These are busy, successful people—you do not want to waste their time. Nonetheless, you want to walk away with information that will help you.

The five questions I asked were:

1. What is the number-one piece of advice you would give me to help me get started?

2. What has been your greatest achievement?

3. What has been your biggest failure?

4. What surprised you the most about going into business for yourself?

5. What are the top three things you would tell me not to do?

The important thing is to be sincere and appreciative. After meeting with the individuals, always send a well-written thank you note.

Step Two: Find the Money

Many businesses fail during the first year because of money problems, especially because of overspending and not having enough cash reserve. I encourage you to have a strong business plan and stick to it.

Every person I interviewed told me to have at least six months to a year's worth of living expenses in a business account. That money is above and beyond what you will spend in setting up the office and your business. I cannot emphasize enough how important this is. This is your lifeline; you will not survive without it.

Be very clear on what you need to survive each month. I have had clients that did not pay for 120 days. This is a long time to wait for money.

Be smart with the money you do have to get started. A friend left a law firm to move into consulting. He got a great loan from the bank, but instead of starting small, he started big. He had big offices, too many conference rooms and expensive advertising. After 18 months, he had to go out of business. The biggest problem was cash flow. The message: Start small and build.

Step Three: Set Up the Office

If you feel sure your have the right amount of money, and you have the answers to the five questions you asked, it is time to move forward into your new venture. First, let's think about your office. Some questions to ask yourself:

• Will clients come to my office?

• Will I have staff? Do I need a separate office for them?

• Can I have an office in my home?

If you do need an office outside your home:

• How much space do I really need?

• How much can I afford?

• How accessible is it to my clients?

• Is it in a good location?

Step Four: Get Equipment

Once the office space is determined, the furniture and equipment come next. While your budget can really be impacted here, it is important to have everything you need. You cannot skimp on this since you will be using your equipment on a daily basis. Invest in the best you can afford. Here are what I call "the essentials":

• A computer

• A comfortable chair

• A functional desk

• A good lamp

• A copier/printer/scanner/fax machine

• A paper shredder

• File cabinets

• Wastepaper baskets

• A landline with a speakerphone and a headset

These days, when everyone uses cell phones, it sounds antiquated to say get a good landline phone for your office. I will risk sounding antiquated. You need to have a phone that works when there is a storm or bad weather. You need to have a speakerphone for times when you have someone else in your office whom you want to include in a conversation. You need a headset so you can take notes when you need to use both hands.

Step Five: Get Supplies

Once you have made all the decisions about equipment, it is time to think about supplies. Coming from corporate America, I took too many things for granted. There, I always had everything I needed;

I did not have to think about it. However, when I set up my own office, I quickly learned that supplies did not magically appear. You need to buy plenty of everything. You will be so busy you do not want to run out of paper or printer ink in the middle of preparing a proposal or responding to a request from a client. Set up a storage closet that has everything you need at your fingertips.

Now it is beginning to look and feel like an office. You have started laying the foundation. Still, you have many more things to do before you can open the door and say, "I am in business!"

Step Six: Create a Brand

Have you developed a logo? Have you applied for a domain name? Do you already have a website? It takes time and planning and this is all part of the strategy to help you get through the maze.

- **Website.** You must have a professionally designed website. It tells the world what you do and how you do it and gives them a visual snapshot of you and your business. You will need a good, professional headshot for your website, information sheets about your products and services, as well as brochures and fact sheets for newspaper stories or interviews.

- **Photos.** Keep photographs current. Women may need to have photos taken more frequently to keep up with styles. I recently scheduled a meeting with someone new and went to her website to see what she looked like. I was sitting in a coffee shop waiting for her when a woman came up to me and said, "Hello." The woman greeting me did not look at all like her photo on the website. She was at least ten years older and had changed her hair color. I would never have found her in the coffee shop. Thank goodness, she found me. Make sure you and your photo match!

- **Stationery.** You will need stationery with a good-looking letterhead that includes your logo and that you can use both on the computer and for handwritten letters.

- **Business cards.** Business cards are essential. Make the information clear and easy to read. I have received cards for which you need a magnifying glass to read the information. I have gotten cards so big that they do not fit any Rolodex® or business card holder. Make it easy on the person receiving your card. It should have your name, the name of your business, your title, your address, your phone number or numbers, your email address and your website. Two-sided business cards have become very popular. You can use the back to describe your business, your purpose or your services. Photos on cards have also become quite popular. It is all personal preference, but it must look professional and make a good first impression.

- **Get connected online.** Join all the social media groups that will benefit your business and that you have time to keep up. Among the most popular right now are LinkedIn®, Facebook® and Twitter®. By next year, there will be many more. Join as many as you need to establish and maintain a web presence. Remember to keep what you post on these sites consistent with your brand and image.

Step Seven: Announce the Happy Event!

Once you have completed all your pre-work, it is time to send a formal announcement to your mailing list, your friends and connections in your online social networks, everyone in your hard copy or electronic address book and Rolodex, your holiday card list and personal address book. Your announcement should include everything: the name of your business, what service or product you provide, your website, your telephone numbers, your email address and your photo. You are the product, and your network will help get the information out. See if you can get a newspaper story about your business or a mention in a column. The more people who know about you and your business, the better.

Now It Is Time to Get to Work

You are in business. Now, it is time to really get to work. It does not matter if you are a sole proprietor or have employees, your days of working a forty-hour week are over. Prepare yourself for sixty- or eighty-hour weeks. In some ways, you work all the time. You are now a business owner. You have to establish and maintain that brand. Everywhere you go, everyone you talk to, every meeting you attend, you present yourself as a business owner.

Study the Marketplace

Get to know your competition. Research everyone in your area who is offering the same or similar service. Find out everything you can about them. What is the going rate for the service or services you provide? Are you pricing your services competitively? Are there too many people offering the same service?

Determine who your clients will be and learn their needs, wants and spending power. Clients love it when you know about them, when they don't have to spend time explaining who they are. Impress them with your knowledge and the fact that you have done your homework.

Set goals. Where do you want to be in three months, six months, a year?

Network and Work Your Net

This is not the time to sit in your office; this is the time to be seen and heard. Go to networking meetings, join the local chamber of commerce and professional organizations related to your product or service. Meet people for breakfast, lunch and dinner. Volunteer to speak to organizations. Make cold calls to your client base. At every opportunity, get your brand out there. Build your network, and you will build your company.

Wear Many Hats

Regardless of your chosen business, or whether or not you have staff, you wear many hats as a business owner. At any time, you may be the receptionist, the secretary, the finance department, the human resources department and the public relations group. You are responsible for each of those functions. Here are tips to help you in these roles:

- Answer the telephone with a smile.

- Return phone calls as soon as possible.

- Respond to emails several times a day.

- Check your spelling and grammar before sending or mailing anything.

- Send invoices immediately after doing the work.

- Use letterhead with your logo on the invoice.

- Gather all receipts daily and file them in a folder.

- Keep track of all business expenses and receipts.

- Make a commitment to keeping your financial records in order. Obtain financial software such as Quicken® or contract with a bookkeeper.

• Write thank you notes to everyone with whom you do business.

• Write notes to follow up with people you meet at networking meetings.

• Keep your website current and updated regularly.

• Keep up with your social networks almost daily.

You are the best PR for your company. Walk the walk and talk the talk. Constantly keep your brand out there. You have a responsibility to your company, your name, your future.

Ask for Help

A mistake many people who go into business make is not asking for help. To get through the maze, you must be willing to ask for help when you "hit the wall." It is okay. It is often necessary. You are not a failure because you are asking for help. I urge you to ask. Go back to that group I suggested you interview at the beginning, seek advice from friends and create a support group or an advisory board.

Keep Current

To be competitive, you have to know what is happening in your industry: what is changing, what the trends are, who the experts are. Subscribe to newspapers or read online papers. It does not matter how you do it, but you cannot be left behind. It is a time of constant change.

Believe in Yourself

Believe in yourself and your business. You are the product; you are the best advertisement for what you sell. People will pick up your energy.

If you believe in yourself, people will believe in you. You have to be your own best support system. You made the decision to go into business, and you must believe you can do it.

This is the beginning of understanding how to get through the maze of starting a business. Keep studying and developing more maze brightness in every phase of your business. The hard work it takes to get started will pay off in the end. You need to know where you are going and assure yourself of ending up in the right place. You want to have maze brightness. There is no greater reward than navigating the maze and coming out with a thriving, successful business.

SYLVIA A. STERN
Re-Image by Sylvia

Helping individuals and companies move from "what is" to "what can be"

(512) 302-4078
sylvia@reimagebysylvia.com
www.re-imagebysylvia.com

Sylvia is a communication and branding strategist with more than 25 years of experience in management, leadership and communication. She is skilled in assessing a situation and then producing a creative, effective and practical plan to achieve success. Sylvia has coached and guided men and women to help them improve professional and personal workplace issues in order to produce the best possible results. She has worked with powerhouse corporations, such as IBM®, Dell® and Radio Shack®, small businesses, universities, hospitals and nonprofits.

As a former corporate executive, Sylvia brings her extensive business experience to her work. A lively and energetic speaker and trainer, Sylvia develops and delivers workshops, facilitates focus groups and provides one-on-one coaching in the areas of communication, leadership, change and branding.

Sylvia is a professional trainer and a popular keynote speaker. She has given more than 500 presentations to audiences in more than 30 states and Puerto Rico. She has a bachelor of arts in communications and a master of science in psychology.

Your Business Guidance System

How Purpose, Values, Vision and Mission Maximize Your Results

By Sylvia Dolena and Pat Duran

As a savvy business person, you probably know how to create a motivating purpose, set of values, compelling vision and mission for your business. You probably know that most business books, business education and leadership gurus recommend that every business have them. Knowing it and doing it are universes apart. Many business owners, especially entrepreneurs and sole proprietors, believe they can hold all of it in their heads. When the company grows, typically the purpose, values, vision and mission are left behind.

In the book *Built to Last*, published in 2004 by HarperCollins, authors Jim Collins and Jerry Porras reported that a common element in long-lived, successful companies is their core ideology—core values and a purpose that guide the company through thick and thin. Two other elements common to these companies are the BHAGs—big, hairy, audacious goals—and an exciting, compelling vision. These elements—purpose, values, vision and mission—comprise your Business Guidance System (BGS).

We have worked with hundreds of huge to small organizations, many of which were in trouble because they did not develop a strong, powerful BGS to guide and support the future growth of their business.

Your BGS

Life's most important questions are these:

• Why do you exist?

• What do you stand for and how do you relate with others?

• What does your future look like?

• What are you going to accomplish?

When you answer these questions for yourself, you know who you are and where you are going. It is the same for your business.

BGS is an organizing principle and a driving force. It unites people in a cause and motivates coordinated action. Your BGS clearly defines the important aspects of your business and where you are taking it. Like a GPS, vision and mission show you where you are, your destination and how to get there. More than a GPS, your purpose keeps you motivated with "why" you are in business. Values are your "rules of the road" as you and your team relate to each other, to your partners and to customers. Together, these elements are a way of maneuvering and navigating your business toward success.

The Power of Your BGS

Clarity. When you know why you exist, where you are going and what you must accomplish, you become aware of the impact of your actions and feel responsible for them.

Decision-making. Whenever an important decision needs to be made, you can refer to your BGS, and one option will be more clearly aligned with your BGS than others.

Unity and alignment. Your BGS unites and aligns your team so its members are all working toward the same end. This can make the difference between making a profit and a losing situation. Even if you only have two people on your team, you both need to be going in the same direction.

Passion. When your team members know how their specific efforts contribute to the end result, they get motivated and excited. Passion comes from knowing the "why" and being able to picture the outcome.

Momentum. "Just put me in, Coach!" That kind of energy and passion creates a momentum that is unstoppable. When your team is excited and involved, that momentum accomplishes goals quickly.

Values-based. There is nothing more attractive to customers and clients than knowing they can count on a business to operate consistently with integrity and the values you deem important to you and your business.

Creating Your BGS

Start with Your Purpose

Purpose answers the question: "Why do you as a business exist?" Every business must make money. However, purpose defines the basic customer needs your business exists to fulfill. It is the single most important component of your BGS. A well-developed purpose provides long-term continuity as the business operates over time. A purpose is not associated with a definitive end point, time frame or deadline. Unlike a mission or vision, which can change, a purpose does not change unless the actual nature of the business changes.

Here is an example of the power of purpose. A client was having a difficult time making enough profit in her business to quit her part-time job. As a result, she was stressed and overworked. She questioned whether she did the right thing in starting this business. We asked her to think back to the time when she first had the idea for her business. What was exciting and motivating about it? Why does her business exist? Her face lit up when she recalled her reason for starting the business. She wrote down her purpose and said, "I'm carrying this statement of purpose around with me everywhere." Within three months, her business became more profitable. Was it because she wrote down her purpose? Of course not! It was because she remembered all the reasons that motivated her in the beginning and that was enough to keep her going.

A well-formed purpose:

• Answers the question "Why do you exist?" in a broad, yet focused, way.

• Clearly conveys the fundamental human need you are fulfilling.

• Is simple enough for your grandmother to understand.

• Is broad, fundamental, inspirational, enduring, compelling and overarching enough to last for decades.

Our Accelerated Women Entrepreneurs™ (AWE) company purpose is "To help people create the work they love." The work they love can be a job, a career, a for-profit business or a nonprofit business. In early 2009, we focused our workshops and coaching on people who lost their jobs and were transitioning into a new position. When jobs became scarce, we focused on helping entrepreneurs start their own businesses. Our purpose stayed the same. Our mission changed due to changes in the economic environment.

Here are some examples of business purposes, two from two-person companies and one from a large corporation.

- *To provide unparalleled edu-tainment*—Hawaiian Cinema Productions™

- *To help corporations succeed through mid-tier leadership development* —Preston Leadership™

- *To give unlimited opportunity to women* —Mary Kay®

There are many ways to create your purpose statement. Here is one way that is effective whether you are doing this alone or with a group.

1. Brainstorm a list of reasons you exist. Begin the phrase with "My business exists to _____." Keep repeating this phrase with whatever comes to mind until you cannot think of any more responses.

2. Organize the list into whatever natural categories you notice. As you place the phrases under a category, position them in a hierarchy of most important to least important to you and your team. For us, the categories were Job/Career, Business, Teaching/Coaching.

3. Look for common threads across the categories. For us, the threads were "help people," "find or create work" and "something people dreamed about or desired."

4. From those threads, create your purpose statement. Say your purpose out loud. Does it ring true for you? Does it feel right? When we said out loud, "Our purpose is to *help people create the work they love,*" we said, "Yes, that's it!"

With purpose as your foundation, you can then develop the rest of your BGS.

Clarifying Your Values

Occasionally, we have an opportunity to study a successful team in order to identify their "secret sauce." Inevitably, we discover one of the key ingredients is a strong value system. These teams identify their values and use them to guide and impact every aspect of their business.

Values are what really matters to you—the traits or qualities you hold sacred. High-performing teams have common values, such as customer focus, achievement, accountability, integrity, responsiveness, teamwork, communications, trust, respect and optimizing for the whole. Our AWE values also include passion, freedom and positive attitude. You readily see some companies' values. Consider Nordstrom®'s customer service or Apple®'s ease of use and innovation.

A common mistake small business owners make is to leave their values implicit, as unwritten rules, of which people may or may not be aware. Make your values explicit, and they will guide your team.

To develop your team values:

• Collect the values that each member of your team holds dear. Ask questions to determine what is important to you in different situations, such as when you are at your best, when you are upset and when you are admiring someone. Be sure to include ubiquitous values, those that are so ingrained you do not even notice them. For example, a teacher might forget to mention learning.

• Cluster and label the values.

- Describe each value as behaviors to develop a shared understanding. For example, "*collaboration* means people working together toward solutions" and "*integrity* means doing what we say, both inside and outside the company."

- Review, revise and gain agreement.

Another common mistake of small business owners is behaving contrary to their values. If you value customer satisfaction, reward people who deliver the kind of customer service you want rather than the fastest turnaround. In business, as in life, "Actions speak louder than words."

What Is Your Vision?

A vision is a vivid, compelling description of the desired future state of your business. It touches people deeply, moves them to action and creates a shared understanding of what it will be like when your business is working the way you want it to.

Your purpose describes the reason for existence; vision provides direction. Consider a tutor whose purpose is to provide affordable, high-tech education. His business will be very different depending on whether his vision is to have computer-equipped classrooms throughout the country or to make home visits.

Your vision can be as long as ten years from the present, but usually is one to three years from the present. You can have a vision for your entire business or for any organization within your business. To be complete, your vision will include perspectives from your customers, suppliers, partners, team members and competitors.

Since the vision description can be several paragraphs long, create a vision statement, a shorter summary of your vision, for easy communication. Here is our AWE vision statement: *Boosting the economy one successful business at a time.*

Here are some sample vision statements, one from a large corporation, one from a two-person start-up and one from a team:

• Empowering people through great software anytime, any place and on any device —Microsoft®

• Our compelling documentary films are the catalyst for social and economic change in Hawaii —Hawaiian Cinema Productions™

• Product of Choice, Partner of Choice, Place of Choice —product development team in Hewlett-Packard®.

A well-written, well-communicated vision can be powerful. A newly-formed team was in trouble. The team members were drawn from four other teams who had previously competed with one another. They knew their purpose, but they were going in different directions based on allegiance to their previous teams.

We recommended developing a vision and mission. The team's name was based on *The Wizard of Oz,* and we decided to use the story as a metaphor. This was ideal since the story had a journey, a wicked witch and four main characters to represent the four previous teams. The team immediately saw the value of linking the wicked witch to outside competition rather than their teammates. They laughed together and had fun tying in the metaphor. They developed a skit, customized the songs, rented costumes and some theatre pieces, and enacted their vision. The team members aligned easily with the vision and started using the metaphor in everyday conversations—they had internalized their vision. The result? They accomplished their mission and developed *three times as many products in a shorter time frame and under budget.*

Developing a compelling vision is a creative process that guides you to access your deep desires and often uncovers features of which you were not consciously aware. Getting into the appropriate mental state is important, so preparation is key. Your company vision may start out vague and unaligned, unique to each individual. You will develop clarity and alignment with each step of the process.

Your preparation includes:

1. Explore industry trends, future customer requirements, business directions, technology advances and group values. Review your purpose.

2. Decide on a time frame for your vision—generally, one to three years out.

3. Explore what questions you want to answer or address in your vision. Include questions about your clients, contribution, partners, suppliers, reputation, culture, work practices, organization, management style and communications—what you are doing, what people are saying about you, and why people want to work here.

4. Decide which perspectives you want to explore in your vision. Possibilities include team members, customers, partners, suppliers, industry specialists and competitors. You will step into the shoes of these people and view the future from their perspective, for example, how your customers are experiencing your business in the future.

5. Decide who will facilitate the meeting. It is difficult to be creative *and* guide the process.

Here is one way to develop your vision:

• Start the meeting with a creativity warm-up exercise. See any of the multiple websites on creativity exercises, such as www. creativethinkingwith.com/Creative-Thinking-Exercises.html.

- Step into the future. Imagine you could wave a magic wand—or use a time machine or whatever device works for you—and be in the future. Explore it with the questions you developed in step three of the preparation and from the perspectives you identified in step four of the preparation.

- Create statements, stories, metaphors and pictures that capture the ideas.

- Make your vision clear, aligned and compelling.

- Share it with key people and refine it.

Qualities of a well-formed vision:

- **Sensory specific.** Describe what people are doing and saying, the sights, movement, colors, sounds and feelings. Make it real. For example, "Customers are streaming through our doors and have big smiles on their faces. They say, 'My business and my life have transformed as a result of working with you,' and they tell all their friends about us."

- **Emotional.** Describe how you will *feel*. Reflect your passion, emotion and convictions. For example, "I feel fulfilled, excited and eager to get to work every morning."

- **Stated in the positive.** Describe what you want, not what you do not want. Instead of saying "No more customer complaints," say "Rave reviews from customers."

- **Present tense.** Instead of "We *would* have many clients," say, "We *have* many clients."

- **An ambitious stretch and within your power to achieve.** Imagine stretching a rubber band with the vision at the top and the current state at the bottom. The vision should be a stretch that draws the current state toward it—not so far out that it breaks the rubber band, nor too close that it creates slack.

When you apply all the above, your vision will create excitement, energy and optimism while giving your business direction and focus. Update your vision as you achieve pieces of it and as your priorities and environment change. You want to maintain the proper amount of creative tension—remember the rubber band analogy—to keep your vision motivating. We recommend a refresh at least annually.

What Is Your Mission?

Mission answers the question: "What are you going to accomplish?" A mission is a stretch project with goals meant to challenge you, yet be realistic and achievable. Your mission focuses time, effort and resources to make significant progress toward your vision. It helps you set correct priorities and make appropriate decisions. For example, our AWE mission is "Support 200 entrepreneurs through the Vision into Action process within 24 months."

Examples of mission statements include:

• Produce an award-winning documentary film within two years.

• Increase customer satisfaction to a score of 9.5 on the customer survey within 12 months.

• Increase sales by fifteen percent in Q2.

• Put a man on the moon by the end of the decade.

Steps to create your mission include:

• Develop a clear and compelling goal that makes progress toward your vision.

- Set a specific end point and time frame for achievement.

- Define the qualitative and quantitative outcomes.

- Develop strategies, actions and tasks and break down the mission into small, actionable steps.

- Put milestones, checkpoints and measures in place to keep you on track.

You may require multiple missions to achieve your vision. Stay focused on the current mission and, as you make progress, start planning the next one.

How to Align Your BGS

Ask yourself these questions and notice any gaps or incongruence:

- Is your purpose truly why you exist? Purpose is your stake in the ground. All other components align to purpose. Ensure it is compelling, clear and comprehensive.

- Is your vision a bigger-than-life expression of your purpose? Step into your future vision and ask yourself, if this is all I ever do, was I true to my business purpose?

- When your mission is accomplished, are you significantly closer to your vision? Are there any deviations or gaps? Will you need to make course corrections along the way?

- When you live and practice your values, do they help you operate effectively as you move toward your vision? Are there any conflicting values when you consider purpose, vision and mission?

Communicating Your BGS

The most important aspect of communicating your BGS is walking the talk. You *must* live it because this is the only way people will believe you. Share stories about your BGS, make decisions based on your BGS and demonstrate it in your behavior. That is a sign of integrity, which is most likely one of your values. What you think, what you say, and how you act are all aligned with your BGS.

Half the journey to success is knowing where you want to go and why. The other half is figuring out how to get there. When you create your BGS, you have both halves covered. You can now take action with confidence. If not now, *when?*

SYLVIA DOLENA AND PAT DURAN
Founders
Accelerated Women Entrepreneurs™

(408) 972-1200
info@awentrepreneur.com
www.awentrepreneur.com

Pat (on left) and Sylvia founded Accelerated Women Entrepreneurs (AWE) to help people create the work they love. As internal consultants at Hewlett-Packard® (HP), they helped HP groups start new ventures and improve existing ones. Essential to that consulting was helping create Business Guidance Systems (BGSs) and implement strategic plans. Their blend of business savvy and interpersonal dynamics resulted in long-lasting changes.

Before, during and after their time at HP, Sylvia and Pat both started their own companies in business consulting, software engineering consulting, real estate investing, farming, film production, retail and coaching. They have helped start hundreds of small businesses in California and Hawaii. They have worked internationally, teaching more than 300 workshops and leading teams focused on business improvement and business creation. Their passion is to build community for people to succeed together.

Sylvia has two executive master of business administration degrees from the University of Southern California and Stanford University/ IESE, an executive coaching certification and a master consultant certification. She is also a Winning Edge educator.

Pat is an NLP Master Practitioner, Certified Dream Coach®, Certified NLP Coach, Licensed True Purpose® Coach and Certified Too Young to Retire® Coach.

Business Planning—
The Road to Success
By Sheri Cockrell

Y ou are thrilled and unable to contain the excitement you feel—that feeling when you first make the decision to become a business owner and take the steps to turn it into reality. I felt the same exhilaration when I started my first business. It felt like I had finally found what I was meant to do. The excitement lasted until the first time I had to make a major decision about what step to take next—and reality set in. Remember the saying, "If I only knew then what I know now"? I think whoever coined that phrase might have been in business at some point. I want you to avoid some of the trials and errors I made and go for the successes! Here are my secrets to successfully owning an incredible business. It all starts with planning.

Plan Your Way to Success

Why did you start your business? Maybe you identified a need that is not currently being met in the marketplace, maybe you have a talent to share, or you want a second income, better lifestyle or different job. Knowing why you want to be in business is important, but without actual business knowledge, it can lead to a false sense of proficiency. The statistics are grim: In 2009, the Small Business Administration reported that seven out of every ten small businesses survive at least two years and about half of those survive about five years. The cause: lack of skills, knowledge and planning. I want you to become one of the businesses that survive and thrive for years to come.

Business planning is a process that incorporates knowledge and skills. You take big categories such as customer service, legal, product development, bookkeeping, finance, ethics, community service, events, organization, brand and image development, advertising, management and networking and produce a workable outcome. Some of my clients are overwhelmed when they see how many areas are involved in running a business. The bonus to business planning is realizing you do not have to know it all or do it all! Planning simply shrinks the categories into distinct steps and allows you to recognize your strengths and weaknesses and which areas to delegate. This chapter covers the most critical steps.

> *"Plans are only good intentions unless they immediately generate into hard work."*
> —Peter Drucker, Austrian author, management consultant

It All Starts with a Business Plan

You usually create a business plan before you obtain your business license because it takes time to develop. However, you still can and have to do this step even if you are already in business. A business plan is a detailed, step-by-step road map of a one- to three-year growth plan for your business. It is your how-to, what-now and what-if manual. It allows you to understand the whole concept of your company, your mission, vision and why you exist. The format of your business plan, whether informal or formal, is not something you develop overnight and put away. You will go over it many times and set new goals as you and your business grow.

You can hire a professional company to develop the plan for you, but the information you gather and the research it takes to develop it is what you personally will need to build a successful business. If you do not take the time to develop it yourself, you may as well hire the same company to run your business, too. You are the owner and operator. You are financially liable and accountable for every decision that is made for your business. If you do not have the initiative to want to write your own plan, you might not have the initiative to run your own business.

An *informal* business plan will include:

- The name of your company
- The legal structure and owner(s)
- What do I want my business to accomplish?
- The location and its accessibility
- Your licenses and permits
- Who your customers are; your market and niche
- What are the products and or services you offer?
- How you will promote your business and sell your products or services to create cash flow
- Who your competition is and how you are unique

If you are looking to raise capital for your venture, you will show a *formal* business plan to lenders and include financial information, your pricing strategies, suppliers, inventory, equipment, duties and hours of operation. Your business plan will also include information about your need for employees and their skill levels, and what types of insurance you need.

The more you research, the more complete your knowledge will be of your business and its operations. You can see how investigation and research can be a huge benefit toward the success of your business.

Pulling It All Together

Analyze your business, piece by piece, using the inner and outer view of SWOT analysis. This constant process changes as you reach your goals. SWOT analysis, devised by Albert S. Humphrey, a leader in business and management consultation, is one technique I use. I find that this works well when carrying out and initiating ways to do business. Here is how it works:

Strengths. What positive skills do you bring to your business? Strengths can be the quality of the product or service, knowing the cost of production, your knowledge of your customer, how you will distribute and price your product to create profit and so on.

Weaknesses. This is where you have to remove yourself emotionally. Understanding where you need help and being able to ask for it can help you avoid time-wasting, costly mistakes. This can be any area where you need more training, education or practice, such as time management, delegation, budgeting. On the other hand, it could be an area where you need to bring in outside expertise, such as marketing, getting your name out and building customer loyalty.

Opportunities. This area helps you to keep your eyes open for new ways to create revenue streams, such as selling on the Internet, responding to changes in customer's tastes, taking advantage of a competitor's business closing, updating an existing product, and so on.

Threats. Keep your eyes open to threats, such as technology making your product obsolete, changes in customers' tastes, the opening of a competitor's business and so on.

Using SWOT analysis adds layers of value and knowledge to your planning process and allows you to strategize and implement solutions.

Strategizing and Implementing

While it is important to offer good products or services, you also want to concentrate on ways of displaying your business. Strategic planning looks at your future direction and how to take present action. One specific area is customer service.

Customer Service and Planning

Business planning is critical to excellent customer service. You need to know who your customers are, where to find them and how to get your product to them. You want to present customers with a smooth-running business machine that handles their needs, concerns and issues and that creates a lasting relationship. For more on customer service, see page 135 for Victoria Ashford's chapter *From Not to Hot! Creating Sensational Customer Service Inside and Out.*

Stay on top of every area of your business. There is nothing better for a consumer than having a sharp, knowledgeable owner or store clerk who knows the price of every product, whether it is in stock and when they can deliver it. Regularly ask customers to complete surveys on how you are doing and pay close attention to their answers.

The most common questions asked in strategic planning are:

- What do I do?
- What are my mission and my vision?
- For whom am I doing this?
- How can I add value for the customer?
- How do I get customers and how do I get products and services to them?
- How do I position myself above my competitors?

Take some time now to answer these questions.

Implementation comes when you create action plans with budgets, marketing and advertising campaigns and promotions that best connect you to your customers.

Handling the Emotional Side of Business

Our emotions and personal characteristics play a big role in how we work our business. The following personal attributes can help to make an entrepreneur more successful. I have always found that if you know the meaning of an action, it will help you to avoid that action or use it to the best of your ability.

Success-building attributes:

- **Patience:** lack of complaint, tolerance and fortitude
- **Faith:** confidence, trust, reliance, assurance and belief
- **Integrity:** truth, honor, reliability and uprightness
- **Humility:** humbleness, modesty and an unassuming nature
- **Genuineness:** real, legitimate, authentic and true
- **Honesty:** sincerity, truthfulness, openness and candor
- **Confidence:** poise, assurance and self-belief
- **Altruism:** unselfish, humane and philanthropic
- **Assertiveness:** self-confident, self-assured and firm
- **Courage:** brave, daring, gutsy and spirited

Embracing the above characteristics will place the focus on your customers. Embodying theses attributes will give you a genuine passion to help others and build credibility and trust for your business. They are the keys that keep customers coming back and referring you to others.

What about fear and failure? They are part of the territory if you want to succeed. Successful entrepreneurs welcome failure because they know it brings them that much closer to success, and they listen to and work on their fears. Do not let either stop you.

Warning sign attributes:

- •**Worry**: dread, panic, alarm and anxiety
- •**Faithlessness**: untrustworthy, fickle
- •**Impatience**: annoyance, irritation and edginess
- •**Arrogance**: conceit, egotism, superiority and overconfidence
- •**Selfishness**: self-centered, self-seeking and self-interested
- •**Dishonesty**: lying, deceitful, false, corrupt, insincere and unfair
- •**Doubt**: hesitation, distrust, disbelief, suspicion and skepticism
- •**Intolerance**: narrow-mindedness
- •**Passiveness**: inactive, unreceptive and submissive
- •**Aggressiveness**: forcefulness, antagonism and fierceness
- •**Cowardice**: spineless and weak

If you are experiencing any of these warning signs, you need a mental shift. Your mindset and attitudes are key components to building positive attributes. It takes discipline and time to change the negative into positive, but it is well worth the effort. For more on mindset, see page 65 for Vernice "FlyGirl" Armour's chapter, *A Breakthrough Mentality Creates a Breakthrough Business.*

Creating a Supportive Environment

Who supports you in being successful? Take a good look at whom you allow into your life. Do they inspire you? Are they mostly positive? What is *their* life like?

What are you watching and reading? How many hours each day are you spending on activities that nurture you and your success?

Everything you allow into your daily life will mold the way you feel and think. Surround yourself with like-minded people, listen and learn from highly-successful mentors who have been there, and always strive to be the best person you can be with integrity. This will keep you on the right path professionally and personally. It is said that we attract the type of people we are ourselves. The first thing to do, then, is to look in the mirror.

"A clear vision, backed by definite plans, gives you a tremendous feeling of confidence and personal power."
—Brian Tracy, American entrepreneur and author

Avoiding Myths and Mistakes

Business planning has a lot to do with eliminating waste and frustration. Time is our greatest resource. Understanding the following most common myths and mistakes can help you recognize if you are working for business success or are creating problems. They are accompanied by truths and solutions to keep you headed in the right direction.

Myths and Truths

- **Everyone will love my product or service as much as I do.** Not everyone will feel the same as you do about your business. Approach it on a less emotional level so that you have the right perspective in running your business.

- **Everyone I know and meet will honor, respect and take me seriously because I took a risk.** Some reactions to becoming a business owner will surprise you. Most people will wish you well, but you will definitely get negative responses from people you would never expect. You may have to prove to some that you have a credible, professional business, especially if it is a home-based business. Believe in yourself and your business and develop a tough—but professional—outer skin to cope with the negative reactions you might encounter. Do not take negative reactions personally, and serve your customers' needs before your own.

- **I am the boss, so I can set my own schedule and work whenever I want.** Yes, you do set your own working schedule, but most new businesses require more time than a traditional job. It is your business 24/7.

- **I will have no one to answer to or tell me what to do. I am the boss.** Being the boss brings much responsibility. You are responsible for all expenses, decision-making and creative processes.

- **Owning my own business will make me rich beyond my wildest dreams!** It can happen, but realistically, you might not bring home much personal income for the first two years.

- **My lifestyle will change.** Yes, it will change for the better or worse. You will keep most of the profits, but you are also responsible for all of the debt if you are a sole proprietor. Plan, plan, plan!

Mistakes and Solutions

- **Quitting a paying job to devote all of your time to your new business.** *Never quit a paying job to start a business* unless you have another steady source of income. You will not have the financial security you are used to and will need for your personal debts.

- **Spending too much on supplies, equipment, location and so on.** This will give you the false sense that you are actually working on your business. The only areas for which you need start-up capital are supplies, product and customer service. Create a business and personal budget and always ask if you really need something before you buy it.

- **Your pricing structure is off, and you are charging too little or too much. You underestimate how much capital you will need to operate.** Preparing your business plan will help you to know exactly what your operating costs and pricing structures are.

- **Shooting from the hip and not planning.** This will create chaos for your business. Plan and make lists for three-, six- and twelve-month goals. Have the patience to wait for the right time to move forward.

- **Trying to do too much too soon.** Planning and implementing strategies will curb over-generous, time-eating activities.

Even with planning, there will be times when you feel unsure of what you are doing, and you will want to throw up your hands and walk away. This is normal. When this happens, you need to step away. Take a break, meet someone for coffee, exercise, call a friend, take a walk, do anything but business. Just do not give up. Come back to work with a clear head and review your plans. They are not written in stone. If you feel you need to change an area, change it, but remember your why, listen to your instincts and above all else, listen to your customers!

Planning Makes Perfect

One of the reasons that stops people from realizing their dreams of becoming a business owner is fear of the unknown. Planning every area of your business will give you the confidence and professionalism you need to move forward and carry on every day. It adds perspective, puts you in clear control and saves you money.

> *"If you don't have daily objectives, you qualify as a dreamer."*
> —Zig Ziglar, American self-help author and speaker

Remember, you do not have to know it all! Look for help from those who have been there before you. Take time to read the inspiring stories of successful business owners. You will be empowered by their determination and positive attitudes. There isn't anything else I would rather be doing. I will see you soon—and maybe even read your expert chapter in the next book, inspiring others with your story and expert testimony.

SHERI COCKRELL
Founder, CEO
Women's Business Planning Service

Empower ~ Connect ~ Bloom™

(916) 782-5204
sher223@womensbusinessplanning.com
www.womensbusinessplanning.com

Sheri Cockrell ventured into the world of business ownership with her husband more than 16 years ago and has owned a number of businesses. Growing into a self-made entrepreneur is not easy; unless you take the right steps, you encounter many surprises and avoidable mistakes in owning a business. Sheri has made it her mission to help busy women entrepreneurs by *empower*ing them with business direction and skills, *connect*ing them through bridges of opportunity, and helping them *bloom* through affordable promotional events.

Based in Roseville, California, Sheri has earned many certificates of achievement and appreciation in business and volunteer work. Her faith-based principles and hands-on experience in all areas of business ownership help her clients save time and effort. A speaker, trainer and writer, she gives her clients leading-edge information and education in business and e-commerce to help them remain current with today's business transformations and environment. She is a proud member of eWomenNetwork, Placer Women's Network and the Roseville Chamber of Commerce. God's blessings.

Want to Profit More and Prospect Less?

Achieve MVP Status!™

By Marge Piccini

"Strive not to be a success, but rather to be of value."
—Albert Einstein, German-American physicist
and Nobel Prize winner

I work with accomplished sales professionals and business owners who are frustrated and overwhelmed. They are educated and know their business, but they are stuck. Their goals far exceed their current levels of capacity, and they can't squeeze any more time from a day in order to move forward to achieve them. They wonder why their businesses and their incomes ebb and flow while they work harder and harder to try to get ahead. They are moving at a frenetic pace and wear too many hats while other parts of their life are being affected, such as their relationships and well-being.

How can you create the life you crave from this space and pace? It's this same frustration that led me to the discovery of a way to profit more and prospect less. The process is called *Achieve MVP Status*™. Before I employed this process, I was spending 50 percent of my time prospecting for business and the other 50 percent of my time doing business. Within 24 months of employing this system, I had nearly doubled my income and spent 90 percent of my time doing business and 10 percent of my time managing relationships. The clear-cut *Achieve MVP Status* sales leadership program is easy for any sales professional or business owner to use to drive heightened performance, create measurable results and catapult their business to the next level and beyond.

MVP Status

In sports, the MVP is the most valuable player on a team. As you know, MVPs are paraded upon the shoulders of their peers and publicly recognized as standouts. Everyone knows who the MVPs are. They are revered by their coaches, team and community, and they even get a trophy!

In business, specifically business development, the MVP is the *most valuable partner* to one's clients and business referral partners and achieving MVP status is the premier form of differentiation. It is the most successful way to separate yourself from the crowded field of your competitors and elevate your position to achieve bottom-line results. As a former award-winning mortgage professional, I used this process to effectively stand out among over 20,000 other mortgage professionals in the state of Connecticut. It is true—MVPs profit more and prospect less.

There are nine straightforward components to achieving MVP status. Each begins with a letter in the phrase *MVP status*, and all are central to a particular principle, practice or mindset.

<u>M</u>y Value Phrase

> *"I believe that every person has uniqueness—*
> *something that nobody else has."*
> —Michael Schenker, German musician

You have a unique value. It's your differentiator and the thing about you that sets you apart from your peers and your competition. It is the obvious value that someone receives from interacting with you; it is *not* your product or service. Understanding your unique value is critical, as it is the dynamic that will make your clients want to refer others to you, and it's how you will profit more and prospect less. Generally, your unique value is obvious to everyone but you. If you don't know what your unique value is, I recommend that you poll your clients. They know what they value about you and will be happy to share it with you.

Once you know your unique value, you'll want to use it to your advantage in every conversation you have with prospects and business referral partners. I also recommend using it in your bio and marketing materials, including your website and social marketing profiles. Here's the formula for creating your value phrase.

• Identify those with whom you work.

• State their major challenge.

• State what you help them to do. Be concise.

• State the end result.

For example, my value phrase is:

"I work with sales professionals and business owners who are struggling with overwhelm and unsteady income, and I help them increase their influence and position themselves as the most valuable partner for their clients and business referral partners so they can profit more and prospect less."

See how easy it is? When you use your value phrase, you will be astounded by its effectiveness. Begin writing your own value phrase right now.

Value of a Client

What is just one client worth to you, and why is this important to know? The process of measuring the value of a single client is clearly defined below and this piece of information is essential for business planning. You will be surprised to know that many people do not understand this simple concept, so don't be surprised if I challenge your understanding of the value of a single client in this section. How do you determine the value of a client?

- First, take a look at your average commission earned or net revenue earned per client transaction.

- Next, estimate the frequency of each sale in a one-year period.

- Then, assume that after you achieve MVP status with your clients, you will receive three referrals from each client you serve.

Here's an illustration using the following assumptions:

- Your average commission is $100 and your client buys four times per year.

Assuming each new client (average commission per sale = $100) buys 4 times per year and introduces you to 3 or more new clients.

This powerful visual illustrates the bottom-line value of a single client. As you can clearly see, when you develop a strong relationship with your clients built on value and trust, you also create a constant, flowing cascade of clients.

What's your client value? Use the example to figure it out!

Planning and Mindset

The biggest obstacles to your success are lack of a vision and plan for your business and a compromised mindset. When you create a vision, and plan your strategy and steps to achieve it, you must have a strong belief system in order to make it all happen. It is the holy trinity of business success: vision, plan and belief. You will experience sustained success when all three components are fully engaged.

Strong belief is similar to the phrase *"where there is a will there is a way."* When my clients expressed doubt about their new home purchase going smoothly, I asked them if they believed the house they were purchasing was right for them. As long as they believed in their vision of their family living happily in the new home, it would happen. This is what I refer to as *will*. Their real estate agent, attorney and I took care of the plan to make it happen. We took care of the *way*.

> *"Dreams are like the paints of a great artist. Your dreams are your paints; the world is your canvas. Believing is the brush that converts your dreams into a masterpiece of reality."*
> —Author Unknown

I find that even if you have a good clear vision and plan, the following five beliefs are necessary for you to materialize your goals. A weakness in any one of these beliefs will cause you to continue to struggle.

- **Belief in yourself.** This sounds like a simple thing to do, but it is the number-one reason why people fail. You *must* believe in your ability to serve your clients' needs. Doubts can lead to failure. Pursue the training you need to gain your confidence.

- **Belief in your product or service.** You must believe in your product. When you do, it is evident in your nonverbal communication. Your prospect will discern your belief through your body language, which comprises more than half of your communication.

- **Belief that there are people who need you to deliver your product or service.** These are the people who value your unique contribution. They will not be happy or have nearly the same experience with someone else. They will stop shopping around when they encounter you, and you will be the one to get the call back. Your market will find you based on your unique value.

- **Belief in your vision for your business and your life.** A clear vision helps you to focus on materializing that which you desire. It is critically important that you have two visions, one for your business and one for your life, and that they intersect. Otherwise you will be consumed by one or the other.

- **Belief that you can achieve it!** The belief that you can achieve something is the force that sets it in motion. With the belief that you are worthy of materializing your vision, you will.

"The world stands aside for anyone who knows where he is going."
—David Starr Jordan, American writer

Service

When I took sales out of my job description, my sales took off. Imagine that! I simply replaced the word *sales* with *service* and found that the sale came easily when I focused on the specific needs of my client, not my need for the sale. When you are focused on the sale, you half-listen, and this causes you to miss important details that you could deliver to your prospect. These important details help you to over-deliver in the eyes of your client and create the coveted *WOW!* response, which in turn, adds to the cascade of clients.

Remember to be other-centered and focused on providing value by asking questions, listening intently and delivering the solution that your client needs. See *Beyond the Art of Listening* by Suzanne Zazulak Pedro on page 149 and *From Not to Hot! Creating Sensational Customer Service Inside and Out* by Victoria Ashford on page 135 in this book.

A focus on service should extend beyond your business. Get involved in a nonprofit. There are many ways to get involved such as leading, fundraising and volunteering. Find a role that suits you and serve.

Trust

> *"Trust: a firm belief or confidence in the honesty, integrity, reliability, justice, etc. of another person."*
> —Webster's New World College Dictionary

Trust is an essential component to achieving MVP status and creating a cascade of clients. Trust is defined in many ways. I prefer the definition above. You must be committed to conducting yourself in a manner that is honest, reliable and just, and demonstrate a high level of personal and professional integrity in your communication and actions.

The foundation for building trust is to listen, which is discussed on the next page in *Understand Your Client.*

Authenticity

Be authentic. Be real. Be the best version of yourself you can be and not a copycat version of another top sales person or the person who mentored you. Take the practices, tactics and strategies you have been taught and adapt them to your business in a way that is comfortable for you. You are amazing, and you provide a unique value that your clients are seeking.

Be curious. Take a genuine interest in people and their desires, regardless of whether they can buy from you or advance your career.

Be appreciative. What you appreciate appreciates. Appreciate the time and value people share with you. Appreciate your clients and business referral partners. Express your appreciation verbally and in writing, either through a cordial email message or by sending a card.

Teach

Teach, educate, mentor. You can do this within your organization and outside of your organization. Give anyone you can a hand up. Even though you may think you are still learning, you have a wealth of knowledge and experience to share with others. Help them take the fast track to success, just as your mentors, coaches and this book are helping you.

Understand Your Client

Actively listening to your clients is the foundation for creating trust. Your clients can sense your genuine interest in them and your desire to help them reach their goals and dreams. In other words, you will quickly gain your clients' trust by asking a series of thoughtful questions that focus on helping your clients achieve their ultimate outcome as a result of doing business with you. Listen intently to the responses to your questions.

Listening should comprise eighty percent of your consultation with your client, which leaves twenty percent of the time for talking. Many sales professionals conduct their consultations in the exact opposite manner.

When you help people to reach their goals or achieve their dreams, they are appreciative, and the law of reciprocity sets in. Naturally, and without much consideration, people express their gratitude by sharing their happiness and news of their good fortune with others. They will gladly share you with people in their networks, including their friends, family, colleagues and clients.

<u>S</u>urprise Your Client

Deliver *WOW!* Think of *WOW!* as the polish that will make you sparkle and shine in the eyes of your clients, business referral partners and community. *WOW!* is achieved when you over-deliver. The best and easiest way to over-deliver is to under-promise. In order to do this well, you must know your process and have some level of control over it. For example, let's say that Friday is your deadline, and you know that you will have things wrapped up by Wednesday. Communicate your commitment to meet Friday's deadline with your client and then deliver on Wednesday or Thursday when it suits you best. Your client will be thrilled to have been provided that comforting news and be able to cross that item off of their to-do list. The bottom-line result is peace of mind and an impressed client.

There are many ways you can add sparkle and shine to your process. Take a few minutes to see where you can modify your process and deliver *WOW!* today. Take a moment and list your ideas where you can continue to focus on them regularly.

Differentiate Yourself to Profit More and Prospect Less

Be a standout in the crowded field of your competitors. Use the *Achieve MVP Status* process as your strategic advantage to increase your influence, create profitable relationships and become the *most valuable partner* to your clients, business referral partners and your community...fast!

Bottom line: When you *Achieve MVP Status* you *will* profit more and prospect less. Are you ready to catapult your business to the next level and beyond? Start today and profit tomorrow!

MARGE PICCINI

Be brilliant...in business and in life!

(860) 982-5150
marge@margepiccini.com
www.margepiccini.com

Marge knows first-hand that you can profit more and prospect less. As a former award-winning sales professional for a Fortune 100 company, Marge learned the key to success is authenticity—knowing who you are and the unique value that you deliver, being connected to your passion and purpose and carrying out your dreams and visions for your business and your life.

Marge's keynotes, workshops and group coaching programs train participants to use the *Profit More and Prospect Less™* sales leadership program she designed and implemented with remarkable results. Marge catapulted her success when she nearly doubled her income and significantly increased her repeat and client-referred business within 24 months.

Marge's clients profit from her ability to help them discover their unique value; build, manage and maintain profitable relationships; and create and carry out their visions for their businesses and their lives. In her private coaching practice, Marge helps business leaders create and step into their highest vision of themselves.

The Most Important Number in Your Business

Know It to Multiply Your Profits— or Ignore It and Pay the Price

By Dezi Koster

*I*n conjunction with knowing your fixed overhead costs and your breakeven point, what if there's a number that enables you to maximize the profitability of every decision you make in your business—a number that enables you to optimally leverage how your business performs?

Your company's fixed costs, your breakeven point and this number are all related. If you do not know this and know how they are connected, you will not know how to best leverage your spending and how to exponentially grow your business.

The ability to continuously produce the highest profits is something everybody wants. Then why is it that many small to mid-sized businesses do not know that this number exists, let alone how to use it?

This chapter will show you how to get an incredible edge on your competition by putting a *red-hot tip* into practice. Read this carefully and learn how you can take your business to the next level.

As you probably already know, marketing is the main driver for gaining clients and increasing profits, but do you know how much you can and should be spending on marketing to achieve optimal results? Business owners often do not know how to prioritize their spending and many businesses are seriously under-marketed. In this chapter, we are going to make sure that does not happen to you and your business.

What Is the Most Important Number?

It is called the *Contribution Margin* and it is the amount of revenue remaining when you subtract the total variable costs from the selling price of an item.

To make sure we are on the same page, let's define these two terms.

• **Variable Costs.** The cost of an item, sales commission, delivery charges and any other cost that is tied directly to the item and increases and decreases with the number of items being sold.

• **Contribution Margin.** The difference between the selling price of an item and the variable costs associated with it. It is expressed as a percentage of the selling price of that item.

Remember the Formula:
Selling Price of an Item – Total Variable Costs =
Contribution Margin

If the total variable costs are less than the selling price of your product or service, your contribution margin is the percentage (or amount) of profit you make on each item you sell.

For example, let's say you own a women's clothing store, and the selling price of your most popular dress is $500. The cost for each dress is $250, the sales commission is 5% or $25, and the delivery charge per dress is $10, making the total variable cost on each of these dresses $285 ($250 + $25 + $10= $285). The contribution margin is $215 ($500 - $285 =$215). The amount $215, when divided into $500, equals .43. Calculated as a percentage, your contribution margin is 43% of the selling price ($215 ÷ $500 = .43 x 100 = 43%).

As you track how your sales are progressing over time, your contribution margin can help you determine the selling price you wish to have on future items. Knowing your contribution margin allows you to pinpoint the direction your business is heading, either toward or away from profits at any time. You can now make the necessary adjustments that will keep your business heading in the direction of making profits.

> *"Profit is a reward for being of service to others.*
> *Making more profit is a direct reflection that you are providing*
> *more service. So go out and make more profit with gusto!"*
> — Gordon Bizar, CEO of National Diversified Funding
> Corporation and co-founder of Relight America™

Getting Started

Before you start, do a financial plan so you can determine how much money you have to spend. Your financial plan or budget, as it is sometimes called, is a blueprint for spending and saving future income. It helps you estimate your future income, expenses and assets. As a profit-and-loss statement, it shows how your company is performing over time, the revenues generated, the costs and expenses charged against these revenues and the remaining net income. From this, you can decide how much to spend and save. Your accountant can assist you.

Next, turn your income statement into a contribution income statement (see example below). This statement identifies your fixed and variable costs as separate expenses. Again, your accountant can help you.

Now take a close look at all your expenses. Where can you cut costs without affecting sales? Refine your budget to leverage every dollar you spend. Consider cutting expenses such as:

• The cost of each item you sell

• Any sales commission associated with each item

• Delivery charges associated with each item

Then do the following:

• Enter the selling price for each item.

• Calculate your contribution margin by subtracting the total variable costs from the selling price of each item.

• Do a before-and-after comparison. Once you have calculated your contribution margin, establish a baseline of key factors, such as profits, expenses and sales for the next thirty, sixty and ninety days.

• Begin to make your financial decisions based upon your contribution margin and note how you are increasing your profitability. Compare your previous results to the results you now achieve.

I realize this may be hard to follow, but determining your contribution margin is critical to your profitability. Many entrepreneurs and small business owners do not take the time or make the effort to make these calculations, and they miss a valuable opportunity to increase profits and decrease expenses. Knowing and using your contribution margin can mean the difference between making a profit and incurring a loss. Let's see how this can be used to positively impact your bottom line.

Here is an example using a contribution income statement.

Let's say you own a company that makes $575,000 in sales. Your total variable costs are $366,000. Your contribution margin is 36 percent ($209,000 ÷ $575,000 = .36 x 100 = 36%)

Sales	$575,000
Less variable costs:	
Cost of goods sold	274,000
Sales commissions	75,000
Delivery charges	17,000
Total variable costs	**$366,000**
Contribution margin (36%)	**$209,000**
Less fixed costs:	
Rent	18,000
Depreciation	19,000
Insurance	9,000
Utilities	20,000
Advertising	3,000
Wages	60,000
Payroll taxes	15,000
Total fixed costs	**$144,000**
Net operating income	**$65,000**

Let's assume your company only sells one item. Your contribution margin shows that you have up to an additional 36% of the selling price of that item to spend to increase your sales and earn additional profit.

With this, you can accurately track and assess strategies for increasing profits. For example, you could hire a marketing company that agrees to sell only to *new* customers for a 34% commission on each item they sell. At a cursory glance, this appears to be almost triple what you are currently paying in commissions, which is 13% ($75,000 ÷ $575,000 = .130 x 100 = 13%). However, your contribution margin reveals a more precise picture. This is where knowing your contribution margin pays off.

Your 13% commission is already included as part of your contribution margin and is not included in the expenses associated with your new marketing company since they would be selling only to new customers. You can add this amount back into the contribution margin. On sales made by your new marketing company, your contribution margin will increase from 36% to 49% (13% + 36%). If you deduct their 34% commission, your contribution margin on these new additional sales is 15% (49% - 34%).

You will add $150 to your bottom-line profit with every $1,000 of new and additional sales ($1,000 x 15% = $150). In a year, if your contractor sells another $200,000, you will make $30,000 in profit that previously did not exist. If they sell $2 million, you make another $300,000 in profit. Unless you have to increase your fixed overhead to accommodate an increase in volume, this value will continue to hold true.

Imagine what this would do for your business!

What would be the result of applying a strategy like this that increases your sales and how effectively your company is marketed without costing you anything?

Your sales costs of $78,000 ($75,000 in commissions + $3,000 in advertising) brought in a total of $575,000 in sales.

Each dollar that you save in fixed costs that you spend on sales will not just yield one dollar, it will yield multiple times that amount in revenue.

Here, it yields 7.37 times ($575,000 ÷ $78,000).

If your contribution margin is 36%, taking the saving of $1,000 from your fixed costs and spending it on marketing can produce $7,370 in profit. Your contribution margin of 36% will yield $2,650 (36% of $7,370 = $2,650).

This means you can produce $2.65 in added profit for every dollar you save.

Your company may not be this simple. However, you can still make predictions about how your business will perform with relative accuracy through knowing your contribution margin.

Make a list of where and how you can cut fixed costs, and then apply this strategy to make an exponential gain in net profit.

Your Contribution Margin and Your Budget

Through strategically cutting expenses, you can easily grow your contribution margin, increase marketing and sales and know where you can spend and on what to take your business to the next level and increase profits.

Where can you cut costs without affecting sales? Can you outsource, use alternative options for IT and software support, negotiate lower prices with providers, and so on? With every dollar you save, you can increase marketing to increase sales and net profits.

If your contribution margin shows you are accruing a loss on every additional item you sell, you need a correction strategy to reverse this. You may need to raise your price or put more money into advertising and track this to see if you have increased your sales. You could not make this decision if you did not know your contribution margin. While it may seem counter-intuitive to raise the price, you are actually building a greater perceived value in your product or service when you put more marketing money into it and set a higher price.

When using this strategy, you can test the money you spend in several ways and track them over time to see how they produce results. You can identify where you are getting the best results and invest in these areas. For example, are you paying wages instead of commissions on sales of goods/services? If so, you can:

• Put money into marketing to increase your sales instead of paying wages up front.

• Negotiate commissions or bonuses that will increase your contribution margin.

Knowing your contribution margin can help you decide the best action to take.

Your contribution margin can also help you avoid mistakes because it shows you where you are spending on unnecessary items that could be invested in marketing. It also gives you an accurate picture of your costs and allows you to track them.

Estimating loosely, rather than calculating costs, is never a good idea since you may pay employees, contractors and service providers more than your clients are paying you. In addition, you may miss opportunities to add to your net profit.

Leverage Your Resources—Your Red Hot Tip

When you sell several quality products from different suppliers, how do you optimally leverage your resources, especially if one costs more than the others?

Understanding contribution margin helps you explain to suppliers that are more expensive how they can assist you to *increase* your contribution margin by *reducing* their cost to you. In return, you will market their product(s) more aggressively, which will enable you to sell more, thus *increasing* their volume. This increase will override the decrease in *their* contribution margin—providing they have a reasonable amount of contribution margin remaining—and they will make more money by reducing their price, even though their gross margin is reduced. By teaching your suppliers to understand their contribution margins, they will become more profitable and, in turn, so will you.

By combining forces and replicating this practice, you will become more competitive in the marketplace and can outperform your competition.

Provide a Buffer for Changes that Impact Your Business

Your business may experience seasonal changes in volume, or you may want to spend more money on product development or marketing. Your contribution margin will tell you how much money you can spend without operating at a loss while adapting to the changes in and around your business. If your costs are primarily variable, you can ride out these changes.

Apple® started out as a small business on April 1, 1976. It sold the Apple I® personal computer kit. They were hand-built by Steve Wozniak. Today, Apple has created great success in the marketplace with the iPod®, MacBook Pro®, iPhone® and the iPad®. The company is a great role model for small businesses and demonstrates what is possible. Apple has adapted with the times, developed new products that are cutting edge, staged phenomenal marketing campaigns that create lots of buzz, and is now massively successful as a multibillion dollar company.

By knowing your contribution margin, you know exactly how much financial risk you can take to develop new products, expand your product range, expand the scope of your business and take advantage of a rapidly changing market environment.

The Secret to Long-Term Business Success

Your contribution margin tells you which direction to move in order to realize higher profitability. When you know your contribution margin, you will see:

- **How to optimally leverage the performance and operation of your business.** A growth in sales translates into an exponential growth in profits. For example, instead of carrying the cost for staff, which includes wages and items such as insurance, overtime and worker's compensation, you can outsource customer service and administrative duties. The money you save can be invested in effective marketing to increase sales and profits.

- **How to track trends over time.** For example, if your total variable costs are greater than your selling price, this highlights the percentage loss on every item you sell. You know immediately what to address to prevent your business from continuing to operate at a loss and can use a correction strategy to reverse this trend and track performance over time.

• **How to prioritize spending.** The focus of spending money in your business should be on increasing your profits. If something does not generate revenue, ask if it is essential to incur this expense now, or can you defer it until later?

It is important to cut both variable and fixed costs where possible. Cutting your variable costs increases your contribution margin. Every saved dollar either drops directly to your bottom line or is available to generate more sales. When you can leverage savings into cutting fixed costs as well, this will have the biggest impact on your business.

Amazon.com®, Inc. was founded in 1994 by John Bezos and was launched online in 1995. It started out as a small business online bookstore, but soon diversified, selling numerous products from CDs and DVDs to electronics, furniture and food.

Amazon was able to cut out the fixed costs associated with a brick-and-mortar business and could offer more titles and products by being online. The company used a brilliant business model of reducing its fixed costs, offering its clients the largest selection of products available and coupled this with clever, effective marketing.

By knowing the functioning of contribution margin and how it can exponentially grow profits, Amazon was able to take this winning combination and skillfully become America's largest online retailer—a multi-billion-dollar business that trades worldwide.

Each dollar that you save in fixed costs that you spend on sales will not just yield one dollar; it will yield multiple times that amount in revenue. For every dollar you save in relation to your fixed costs, you get an exponential gain in your net profit.

Without knowing your contribution margin, you will miss out on being able to apply this to help your business grow.

You have now seen how applying this simple strategy—reducing or deferring your fixed costs and spending that savings on your marketing—helps generate more profit. When you see what this means for your profits, you will be thrilled that you took the time to learn about it and apply it to enhance the profitability of your business.

Always seek advice from your accountant regarding any new strategies you implement to ensure you make the best decision for your situation.

DEZI KOSTER
Redshift Inc.

*Solutions for creating
boundless wealth and success*

(707) 484-2670
dezi@dezikoster.com
www.dezikoster.com

Dezi Koster utilizes innovative strategies for wealth creation, championing businesses to raise capital, develop multiple revenue streams and set up powerful strategic alliances to expand their revenue earning capacity. She has consulted with companies to deliver 75 -100% increases in their net profits within 6 -12 months.

Dezi is one of the founders of Relight America™—a private sector initiative to jumpstart the economy, produce enduring prosperity and restore domestic harmony™.

As an international speaker, coach and author, Dezi pursues one of her greatest passions—coaching individuals and businesses to flourish at their full potential. She is committed to helping people move beyond their boundaries to achieve success and the abundant life they truly desire.

Dezi has a diverse background, which includes psychology, neurolinguistic programming, alternative medicine, Maharishi Ayurveda, business, health and fitness. Drawing on a wealth of experience that spans more than 25 years, Dezi has presented to audiences as large as 2,000 people, and she has achieved outstanding results coaching thousands of individuals and groups worldwide.

A Breakthrough Mentality™
Creates a Breakthrough Business
By Vernice "FlyGirl" Armour, CCS

I found myself pacing the floor in my bathrobe, trying to figure out what I was going to try to do to turn things around. I had just finished reading the book *Blink,* by Malcolm Gladwell, published in 2005 by Little, Brown and Company, in which he talked about a study that stated the mere act of smiling changed the physiology of the body. Okay, I decided to smile. I pulled back my lips and bared my teeth in what was an attempt at smiling. I am sure had anyone seen me in that very moment, they would have quickly turned around and headed in any other direction but mine!

After smiling, I knew I could not stop there. My police and Marine training taught me that specific action must follow any plan in order to achieve success. The action I took in that moment directly resulted in my business completely turning around. A Breakthrough Mentality led me to take the right action at the right time.

Leveraging a Breakthrough Mentality is the process of using innovative thinking to solve your challenges—thinking "outside the cockpit." Imagine sitting inside the cockpit and all the instruments that take you higher, faster, left or right, are all right there at your fingertips. However, the world you are flying in is outside of the cockpit. To maneuver safely, efficiently and successfully, you must find a balance between scanning your instruments inside the cockpit and flying in a world outside the cockpit, because that is where you soar!

By refusing to settle, even in the smallest moments, you will force yourself to design creative ways to accomplish your goals. This type of thought process will break you out from the competition. I tell all my clients, "If you do what average people do, you'll have what average people have. I don't want to be average, do *you?*"

I will take you through a process for mission accomplishment that I used every day while learning to fly my combat aircraft, the AH-1W Super Cobra Attack Helicopter. I call this five-step process your "flight plan" for success. When you follow these steps, you set yourself up for succeeding in the task you have at hand, as well as setting yourself up for success in future missions.

Breakthrough Mentality Tip. The Breakthrough Mentality tip at the end of each step is meant to serve as a *single-thought* wrap-up that harnesses the essence of what you just read.

• Step One—Create your flight plan

• Step Two—Pre-flight

• Step Three—Takeoff!

• Step Four—Execute

• Step Five—Review, recharge, re-attack!

Step One: Create Your Flight Plan

A major decision needs to be made before you take off and fly anywhere. You must decide where you want to go. Where do you see yourself at the end of the action you have decided to take? The question I like to ask myself to get clear is, "What do I *really* want?"

• What do you really want out of your life?

- What do you want for your company?

- What do you want your journey to look like?

- Do you want to take on this particular project and is it working toward your business goals and objectives?

- How do you want to arrive and how do you want to look and feel when you get there?

These questions asked and answered up front can easily increase the enjoyment of your journey in creating your incredible business. Remember, it is okay not to know how you are going to get there in the very beginning. In fact, if your vision or dream is big enough, there is a very good chance you *will not* know how to reach your desired end state, and the answers are just a step away. Once you have the main question of "What you really want" answered, it is time to craft a plan to make it happen. Now, you need to check out the vehicle (your business) that is going to take you there.

It was an exciting journey when I was answering those questions for my life. Seven months before leaving the Marine Corps, I started to lay the foundation for my speaking and coaching business. I already knew that it takes the average business three to five years to show a profit and be successful. I needed to achieve both milestones in my first year in order to pay the bills and take care of my family. In order to do that, I knew I needed to be on the fast track.

As a former police officer and attack helicopter pilot, I knew all about chasing a criminal or flying over the desert at 300 feet shooting missiles, but running a business was foreign to me. I formulated a plan based on the dreams I wanted to achieve. The business made over six figures in the first year. Here are the steps to use to create *your* plan:

- Create your vision.

- Ask yourself the right questions.

- Get a coach or mentor.

- Research and join one or two key associations in your industry.

- Find a mentor who is already successful doing what you want to do.

Throughout this chapter, I will reference several exercises I have developed to help you achieve your breakthrough business. To download the worksheets, go to www.vernicearmour.com/worksheets.html. There, you will find resources and tools that will help you create a Breakthrough Mentality and achieve your goals.

> *"One important key to success is self-confidence.*
> *An important key to self-confidence is preparation."*
> —Arthur Ashe, American social activist
> and champion tennis player

Breakthrough Mentality Tip. Prepare for your passion!

Step Two: Pre-Flight

After leaving the ready-room, the place where pilots are briefed before an upcoming mission, they head straight down to get the aircraft ready for flight. They gather up their gear: helmet, maps, kneeboard, flight bag, etc. and walk out to the aircraft and inspect it for hazards. The same process applies to your business.

First, what kind of business are you creating? Check out your business plan. Are you an expert in the industry you have chosen or do you need to do a lot of homework? A Breakthrough Mentality shows itself in how willing you are to get the best mentoring and preparation you can get. Could you benefit from business or other type of industry-specific coaching? What materials, hardware or products do you need to open your doors for business? If you are already in business, what do you need to take your organization to the next level?

Ask individuals who are already successful what their best practices are. Asking someone if you can "pick their brain" is different from honoring your time and theirs by asking specific questions where they can give you specific answers.

This phase of business was absolutely critical for me. After I decided to leave the Marine Corps, I immediately looked for resources to help lay the foundation for my business. I attended my first speaker's training seminar. I joined the National Speakers Association and started networking several times a week in order to let people know I was launching a business. I even booked several speaking presentations to provide real-world experience during the final months of my exit strategy from the Marine Corps.

Continue to look at what you want to achieve. Lay the groundwork for success. Who can you look to for support? What kind of resources do you need around you in order to complete everything you need for success? Can you hire someone for these needs? Are interns a viable option? There are many ways to get started; make sure you are opening yourself up to discovery and "make your break." Opportunities do not go away; other people take advantage of them.

Breakthrough Mentality Tip. Create the exit strategy that works for *you,* pick a date and jump!

Step Three: Take Off

It is time to strap yourself into the cockpit, start your engines and take flight. At this point, you have determined your aircraft (business) is ready to fly. I was talking to a client, and she kept saying things like, "It will be hard, but I'm going to do it. They want me to complete too many requirements. I hope I can make the finals."

Statements like these do not exactly ooze confidence. Get set in your mind that you can do it and act with the confidence of knowing you are prepared. Take action! Take flight.

I completed my preparation phase and moved into the execution phase with a huge bang. I had managed to book six gigs for my first month. Over the next few months, I had a few speaking gigs each month, until November and December. I had nothing scheduled for the coming year. I was terrified! However, I knew I had made the right choice, and I was now "flying." Now, I just needed to figure out how to break through.

Breakthrough Mentality Tip. Who needs a runway? Take off from where you are.

Step Four: Execute

Move into action at 100 percent! Think of the last action movie you watched with the bad guys being chased across rooftops. They are jumping from one building to another. Inevitably, they make a jump where they barely make it to the other side. When the detective gets to that jump, if he hesitates at the looming gap between buildings, what do you think the chances of clearing the gap will be?

Doubts that come up can reinforce your strategy. When the "what if's" arrive, welcome them with the mindset that they are helping you develop a strategy to create a better plan of attack. As soon as you hear the "what if" in your head, train yourself to immediately think of how to mitigate the chances of the "what if" happening, or think how you could create a solution if the "what if" were to happen. How could you realize a positive impact versus a negative result? Doubts can help you build a solid plan.

For example, if Engineer A were to ask Engineer B, "What if the bridge can't hold over 10,000 tons?" All Engineer B has to say is, "Then we can build it with more supports, more steel and a thicker frame." The result from Engineer A's doubts is a stronger bridge that is safer, makes everyone feel better and yields superior results.

"What if the book doesn't sell?" You have two options when this doubt comes up. Create a killer marketing plan, execute and watch your hard work pay off. Then thank the "doubt" for giving you the idea to create the marketing plan. On the other hand, you can remain fearful and do nothing to mitigate the risk.

According to Jeff Olsen in his book *The Slight Edge,* published by Momentum Media in 2005, consistency in your actions, positive or negative, has a profound impact that is compounded over time. For example, if you eat a hamburger today, you will not see a five-pound weight gain tomorrow. If you eat a hamburger every day over six months, it is highly likely that you *will* see a significant weight gain.

Likewise, if you go out and exercise your heart out today, you typically would not see a five-pound weight loss tomorrow. However, if you stayed consistent in your workout regimen, you would more than likely see dramatic results after 60 days.

Many things you need to do to be successful are easy to do, but they are also easy to *not* do! Every decision you make every day needs to drive you toward success. Concentrate on making the small decisions and taking the seemingly small actions every day. This consistency of the everyday breakthrough will compound over time to create the major breakthrough for which you are working so hard.

When I think of this concept, I cannot help but think of Michael Phelps. What one workout, one meal or visual exercise helped him win by a fingertip during one of his record races? Can you imagine winning anything by a fingertip and trying to analyze what one thing gave you the advantage? The answer is it was the sum of everything he did every day.

During this phase, I needed a little push to continue doing what I had started. I had lost sight of follow-up calls when my situation started to get overly challenging. After reflecting on the book *Blink,* referenced at the beginning of the chapter, I made a follow-up call. From that call, I decided to take a risk and drive to a conference hundreds of miles away in hopes of building strategic relationships with clients who would want my services.

By driving hundreds of miles and attending The Women of Color in Technology STEM (Science Technology Engineering Mathematics) Conference, I took a major step into my future.

The relationship building that happened at that conference was phenomenal. Within thirty days, I had speaking engagements lined up with companies like The Boeing Company, Booz Allen Hamilton and Bank of America. To this day, I still get requests to speak at corporations out of a conscious decision to take action, take a risk and attend a conference that I knew had the potential to be good for business.

Harnessing the power of a Breakthrough Mentality means refusing to settle, in even the smallest moments, making the small, seemingly irrelevant decisions that change the world—*your* world—and creating a series of small breakthroughs that make it possible for the big breakthrough to come to fruition.

Breakthrough Mentality Tip. Use the slight edge to your advantage. Take consistent, small steps toward your goal.

Step Five: Review, Recharge, Re-attack

During my combat tours, I flew many times in support of the troops on the ground. After every mission, the crews would land the helos, and we would head back to our ready room and debrief. There was never a perfect mission, and there was always something we learned from the flight that we needed to review and analyze. At the end of my shift, I would head back to my tent to get some sleep and recharge. The next day, I would have the opportunity to do it all over again—re-attack—this time just a little bit better than the last.

In your business, there will be times when you feel like you are in combat. Out of every situation, assess and analyze your successes and your failures. Through this review, you will be able to come up with best practices that really work for you and your business. Make sure to take time off when you need it. You are more productive rested and recharged than when you are worn down and burned out. Then get up, get back out there and do it again—even better!

Breakthrough Mentality Tip. There are only two ways to succeed: the first time or again.

> *"Victory is sweetest when you've known defeat."*
> —Malcolm Forbes, American publisher

Refuse to Settle and Make Your Break!

Refuse to settle, even in the smallest of moments, and demand the life you deserve and for which you are willing to work. Opportunities do not go away; other people take advantage of them. A Breakthrough Mentality truly creates a breakthrough life *and* business! Remember, think outside the cockpit and live to your fullest potential. Someone is going to create a successful business this year, why not you? Someone will make a million dollars this year, why not you? Someone will live the life of their dreams this year. Will it be you? Apply what we have discussed in this chapter, and it just might be *you*.

VERNICE "FLYGIRL" ARMOUR, CCS
VAI Consulting and Training, LLC

A Breakthrough Mentality™
creates a breakthrough business!

(888) 213-0431
vernice@vernicearmour.com
www.vernicearmour.com

As featured on Oprah®, CNN®, NPR® and others, Vernice "FlyGirl" Armour's dynamic presentation and coaching methods have inspired hundreds of organizations and individuals. By harnessing the power of innovation, leadership and imagination, Vernice "*excel*erated" from beat cop to combat pilot in three years. Her most notable accomplishment to date was being recognized as America's first African-American female combat pilot.

Having completed two combat tours in Iraq as an AH-1W Super Cobra Attack Helicopter pilot, Vernice leveraged her experiences into her Zero to Breakthrough™ Success Model, producing more than six figures in revenue within the first 12 months! Through keynotes, individual and group coaching and executive retreats, Vernice takes clients from zero to breakthrough with her unique insights.

Vernice has been recognized with awards as a pioneering pilot and for her commanding role in Science, Technology, Engineering and Mathematics (STEM). Vernice was the first African-American woman on the Nashville Police Department's motorcycle squad, is a two-time titleholder in Camp Pendleton's annual Strongest Warrior Competition and was a running back for the San Diego Sunfire women's professional football team. Vernice is currently working on her first book, *Zero to Breakthrough*™.

How to Have a Royally Organized Office

Clearing Your Clutter! Creating Your Calm!

By Nancy LaMont

"Find the environment where you thrive.
We would probably never have heard of Tiger Woods
if there were no golf courses."
—Robert T. Kiyosaki, American investor and author

Starting a business is opening a door to an entirely different way of earning a living—it is living your dream. You begin living your dream with an idea that drives you forward with one goal in mind: making a living. You have this fantastic idea and jump right in without much, if any, planning. "I can do this!" you say, "and I can make a living at it!" You set up a website and start advertising your skills. You spend hours each day with social networking, read some books to get you started and get some business revenue coming in.

This is a very exciting time in your life, but have you considered your office environment? Have you set up your business office to work with you—for you—not against you? As you increase your clients and the jobs you do in your business, you also increase the amount of hard-copy paperwork as well as digital documents and Internet activity you need to keep track of. You can soon find yourself so involved in building your business that your office space ends up disorganized, cluttered and inefficient.

If this sounds like you, this chapter will guide you in the right direction by giving you ideas to consider and action steps to take that will make you the master of your office, paperwork and computer.

Discover Yourself

Before rushing ahead and making office changes, consider who you are in terms of personality, temperament, strengths, weaknesses, likes, dislikes, habits and stressors. What helps you to function at your best while working in an office environment, and what throws you off course?

In order to create the most efficient office environment for you, write down what you already know about your preferences, explore what you do not know and have fun discovering yourself. It can help to ask for the opinion of a spouse, close friend or co-worker.

How do you discover yourself and learn more about your personality and styles? Do a search on the Internet; visit a library or your local bookstore to find helpful information.

What do personality styles have to do with how people organize differently? Personality styles are the various ways people gather or perceive information, the way information is organized and the way decisions are made.

To be efficient and organized, it is important to determine how your brain, via your personality and learning, processes information coming in and going out. For example, when your systems are set up to process and retrieve information the way your brain processes and retrieves information, you will file and find information in less time and with less frustration.

It can take a while to understand your style, but it is worth the effort.

Here are three popular sites to consider visiting to help you figure it out:

- www.authentichappiness.sas.upenn.edu/Default.aspx

- www.keirsey.com/personalityzone/index.asp

- www.myersbriggs.org

Plan Your Office Layout

Now that you see yourself a little more clearly, it is time to plan and design your office space using the information you have collected about yourself. At this point, you want to consider the size and layout of the space you will use for an office, what furniture you may want or need and the best placement of furniture and equipment.

Starting with the overall space, decide details such as color of the walls, placement of lighting and wall decorations. Make the best use of natural lighting, when possible. Coordinate the placement of your desk, bookshelves, file cabinets and office equipment and office storage. As you plan these details, do not neglect the unused wall space from eye level up, especially if lower level space is very limited. Wall shelves and wall cabinets can become your best office buddies.

For the placement of office equipment, such as the telephone, copier/fax machine, printer, shredder and other smaller standard office equipment, remember to keep the equipment you use most often closer at hand; the lesser used equipment can be farther away from your desk.

A Small Space for an Office?

Having a small space for an office, such as one corner of the room or an empty closet space, can be challenging. It can also be a lot of fun to set up. A small space gives you the opportunity to be creative and unique in designing it.

A few important things to remember are proper lighting and using all the space available, including upward space. Put your personality into the space design. Paint just the wall by your desk a different color than the rest of the room. Why not add your favorite wallpaper or trim around your desk area? Hang a plant from the ceiling, even if it is not real. Personalize your space even more by adding shelves above the desk to the ceiling; place office items on lower shelves where they are easy to reach and use the higher shelves for office storage and family photos.

To save floor space and maximize wall space, try installing pegboard on the wall and the back of the door or inside of the closet doors. Just about anything can be hung on the pegboard, including file holders.

Create Your Hard-Copy Filing System

Two important office systems to create are a system for paper documents and files and one for your digital documents and files. We will consider the hard copy system first, and we will discuss computer documents in the next section.

Take time and special care to design a system that allows you to file and retrieve information quickly. Think about what fits your style, your preference, your way of thinking and recalling. There are many ways to set up filing systems; find the way that works best for you.

How do you want to file your hard-copy documents and folders? Here are some things to consider.

Do you want to file:

- Numerically or alphabetically?

- Oldest in front or in back?

- By category of work or color-coding?

Have you given any thought to filing software programs such as The Paper Tiger®? Visit the www.thepapertiger.com for help.

Are you the type of person who prefers all your files out of sight or do certain documents and folders need to be in plain view? Place folders in plain view on your desk in a stair-step vertical file, rather than a flat file. With flat filing, files are piled on top of each other, and it takes more time to find what you are looking for.

Create Your Electronic Filing System

As the amount of time you spend on your computer and on the Internet increases, so do your e-files. Often, documents are named in a rush with no real thought as to how you will find them again when you need them.

Here are a couple of ideas to consider for managing electronic files and documents:

- Put a date at the beginning of every document you save. This will create consistency and help you find the right document based on the approximate date you created it. Here is an example of how to use a date in document naming: 05.18.10 WebsiteDevelopmentAndHosting.doc.

- Use document names that help you find the file or document you need. The names do not have to form a sentence or even make sense. Just add enough key words so you can easily search for and find the document you want. This will save you valuable time.

Create Your Archive Files

When creating your hard copy and electronic filing systems, set up annual archive files, as well. Archiving occurs at the end of your business year, either annual or fiscal. Here are some examples to help with archiving:

Hard copy folders. First, remove any no-longer-needed folders from your working file drawer and place them in an archive drawer. Now, make new, identical folders to replace those folders you are moving into the archive drawer. Insert the new folders in your working file drawer. Last, create new file folders you will need for the upcoming year and put them in your working file drawer.

Electronic folders. Set up three separate, identical e-folders: one for the current year, one for the previous year, and one for the year ahead. Within each of these annual e-folders, make as many additional e-folders as you need based on the type of documents your business uses, what you need and your style. One common way is to make a folder for each letter of the alphabet A – Z. Place e-documents within these e-folders according to the starting letter in the title after the date. Another popular system is to make e-folders by subjects and place them in the "year" folders. I have set up my client files so that at the end of December of the current year, I move all my current client files that are completed and closed to the archived folder. For example:

- Archived (Folder)

    - ArchivedClients (Folder)

        - xx.xx.xx Client's Name (Month.Day.Year.Name) (Folder)

            - xx.xx.xx Client's Name PhoneConsult (Document)

            - xx.xx.xx Client's Name Assessment (Document)

            - xx.xx.xx Client's Name Signed Document Name

            - xx.xx.xx Client's Name FeedbackForm

        - xx.xx.xx Client's Name (Month.Day.Year.Name) (Folder)

        - xx.xx.xx Client's Name (Month.Day.Year.Name) (Folder)

    - ArchivedTaxReturns (Folder)

As the year ends, remove e-folders that are no longer needed and place them in the archive files. Now, remove any e-documents you will not need regularly and file them in the archive folder. Make new e-folders you will need during the next year.

As you set up your hard copy filing and e-filing systems, think about how often you need to access files during the year—daily, weekly, monthly? Certain files—such as invoices, current client information and bank statements—fall into this category. Other documents, such as tax documents, only need to be accessed quarterly or annually.

Frequently accessed documents need to be filed closest to where you sit and in the front of the file drawer. This is also where you file "hot" folders, also known as "action" or "urgent" folders. Here are a few common examples:

• To Pay

• To Discuss

• To Do

• To Read

• To Fax

• To Scan

• To Write

File documents and folders you need less often in the back of drawers or in a filing cabinet away from your desk. File archives farthest away from your desk. Store them out of your office if you can. This will free up space for things that need to be closer at hand.

Internet Bookmarks

For your favorites or Internet bookmarks, save them with the same consideration as your paper or e-files. Name your Internet bookmarks so you can locate and use them again. You'll save time searching for your favorites each time you want them and stop creating new names for the same favorites. This will improve your productivity.

Only save a favorite bookmark when you are sure you will need to return to it often. If you are not going to use that particular website favorite on a daily or weekly basis, it is better to search for it again when you do need it.

Change the name so it means something to you and is a name you will remember.

Emails

Email overload! Does this sound familiar? What can be done to minimize email overload on our computers as well as those on the receiving end of our sent emails?

- Do your part by using email for brief messages and then follow up via phone to discuss the topic further. Lengthy emails are time consumers and usually leave the recipient with unanswered questions that lead to a phone conversation anyway.

- Always use keywords in the subject line so the recipient knows exactly what the subject is and can then make a better judgment about answering the email.

- If the subject changes over the course of several back-and-forth emails, change the subject line to match the topic.

- When replying to an email, only use "reply to all" if it is necessary that everyone listed needs to hear what you have to say. Most of the time, we can just reply to the sender only.

Back Up!

Back up, back up, back up. One of the most horrifying computer-related things a business owner, or anyone for that matter, can experience is a computer crash and not having a backup of your data. There are numerous ways to back up your hard drive using computer disks, flash drives and online backup.

The easiest, but most costly, is an online backup system that can be set up to back up and run on a regular schedule. You will pay a monthly fee for this service. The good thing about online backups is that your data is safe from being stolen or destroyed in a fire.

Set SMART Goals

The term "SMART goal" was originated in 1981 by George T. Doran, who said, "There's a SMART way to write management's goals and objectives." Arthur F. Miller and James A. Cunningham wrote about it in "How to Avoid Costly Job Mismatches," *Management Review,* November 1981, Volume 70, Issue 11.

Setting SMART goals for working in your office and for staying organized really does help. The first step is to put your goals down in writing. As you write your goals, keep in mind the SMART acronym.

• **Specific**—clearly defined

• **Measurable**—with concrete ways to measure your progress

• **Attainable**—within your reach (with a little stretch)

• **Realistic**—within your ability

• **Timely**—enough time to achieve and has an end date

SMART goals are both long-term and short-term goals. Make a long-term goal for five years out and break it down into many smaller short-term goals. Remember to stay flexible and make changes to your goals as needed.

Make New Habits

When you have an uncluttered desk and efficient filing systems in place, you can locate documents and file folders quickly and effortlessly. Getting and staying organized will increase your productivity. You are less stressed, have fewer embarrassing business problems, save money and time, avoid late fees, eliminate duplicate information and, ultimately, improve your mental and physical health.

The most important, and probably the hardest, step for having a royally organized office is to change current habits that are working against you, and slowly make new habits that work with you and for you.

It is necessary for you to make a few small habit changes—maybe even some major changes! Not making any changes will give you the same old results, but making changes little by little will bring about lasting changes.

As with goals, putting things in writing and keeping them in view will help keep you on track. Now sit back, look around your office space and let the fun begin. To get you started, answer these three questions:

1. How can you set up your office so it serves your business in the best way possible?

2. What electronic and paper files do you need and how will you label them?

3. How are you going to manage email?

Taking time now to set up your office and files can pay huge dividends later by improving your productivity and efficiency. Even if you only have fifteen minutes a day to work on setting yourself up for success, start now to reap positive results and be more productive everyday.

NANCY LAMONT
Bee Royally Organized

Clearing your clutter!
Creating your calm!

(425) 610-6162
nancy@beeroyallyorganized.com
www.beeroyallyorganized.com

Nancy LaMont, owner of Bee Royally Organized, spent over 30 years watching companies struggle with disorganized employees and the resulting loss of clients and money. In April 2008, Nancy launched Bee Royally Organized, a professional organizing company specializing in small business and home-based offices.

Nancy is passionate about coaching small business owners, entrepreneurs and individuals who want to have an efficient office environment. Together they plan, create and implement the right systems that effectively fit into individual business objectives as well as learning and personality styles. She enjoys life as a workshop presenter and organizational speaker, focusing on the benefits of being organized in both business and life.

With a natural flair for organization, Nancy offers a fresh, quality approach to problem solving. She is well known for offering her organizing services at community fundraisers, such as Relay For Life, at local school raffles and at Live Love Laugh for Youth through the Everett Mountaineers. Nancy is a member of the National Association of Professional Organizers (NAPO).

Growing Your Virtual Team
By Joanne Lang

*"No person will make a great business who wants to
do it all himself or get all the credit."*
—Andrew Carnegie, American industrialist and philanthropist

Are you having trouble meeting deadlines? Do administrative tasks get in the way of your revenue-producing activities? If so, you are ready to start building your virtual team so you can continue to do the projects at which you are best, and your clients and customers will keep coming back.

Advantages to Growing a Team

As a business owner, you might believe you can do it alone. Maybe you think that no one can do the projects like you can, or that it takes too much time to delegate. We have all been there. However, what you will find is that, when you delegate, more doors will open for you. It allows you to concentrate on what you do best and to grow both personally and professionally.

You will soon realize that the other people on your team will bring a different perspective and solutions to problems that you have never thought of. As you build your team, you will be adding a knowledge base that includes the experience of each person you bring on board. This can include industry-specific knowledge, process and procedure improvement and increased software capabilities, which can all help you serve your clients better.

Delegating also protects your health. Too much stress may cause or aggravate serious illnesses such as heart disease, stroke and even cancer. If you are overstressed, you cannot give your clients your best. Eventually, it will catch up to you and could damage your business, your health and your personal life.

Many business owners are experiencing more balanced lifestyles as a result of delegating. They tend to take better care of themselves, and they have more time to spend with their families and friends. As a result, they are happier during their workday and are more productive.

What Business Owners Say about Growing a Virtual Team

The following are two business owners who use a virtual assistant (VA) while building their businesses. Here is what they had to say:

"With the help of my virtual assistants, I can get so much more done. As a solopreneur, I am always limited by the time I have available. However, many of the things that need to get done don't actually require me—they are easily delegated to a skilled and trustworthy assistant. Using a VA for these tasks means that I have no overhead for an employee, and I can just use as much time from the assistant as I actually need, and pay only for that. I love having someone to delegate to! It frees up not just my time, but my energy, and allows me to focus on the tasks that only I can do to build my business and offer my services."
—Dinyah Rein, Business Coach and Trainer

"Using a virtual assistant has opened up new sources of client leads. With the help of a VA, my business has moved forward."
—Cari Vinci, franchise consultant

Employee vs. Independent Contractor

One of the benefits of growing a virtual team is that you pay by the hour, project or monthly retainer. You are not committed to an employee and the expenses that go along with having your own staff. Your virtual team is made up of independent contractors. You will not pay for payroll taxes, down time, sick time, vacations or benefits. You also do not have to accommodate someone in your office and pay for additional office equipment or worry about work-related injuries. You just pay your VA the contracted amount to which you agreed in advance for the projects he or she does for you. At the end of the year, you supply the independent contractor with a 1099 form. Please see www.irs.gov for all the requirements.

There are guidelines to follow when choosing an independent contractor. You want to make sure you abide by the law and that the virtual assistant meets all IRS guidelines. Please view the list in its entirety at www.irs.gov. This will minimize the risk to you and your business.

At www.irs.gov, under independent contractors, it states, "The general rule is that an individual is an independent contractor if you, the person for whom the services are performed, have the *right to control or direct only the result of the work and not the means and methods of accomplishing the result.*" Carefully consider this guideline and enlist the help of an experienced consultant if you are unsure if you are following it correctly.

Costs

At first, it is best to get quotes for the project. This way you will have a flat rate with no surprises. Then, you will know how quickly the VA completes his or her work.

See if the VA has a satisfaction guarantee. If the work is not done to your satisfaction, you want to know that he or she will keep working until you are happy, within reason.

The average cost of a virtual assistant is $25 – $50 an hour. The charges are generally different for various projects. For instance, a phone-calling project will be less than a writing project.

Ask for several bids before you pick your virtual assistant, but also factor in how long the VA has been in business, testimonials and how professional the individual's presence is. You want a VA who will stick around for years and is serious about his or her career.

What to Delegate

Now that you know the difference between an employee and an independent contractor, it is time to build your team. Where do you start? First, write down all your challenges. For instance, what projects are not getting done and which deadlines are not being met? Which projects are holding you back from earning more income? Then prioritize your list.

It is common for business owners to generally be very good with the technical aspects of their business and yet need help with their marketing and administrative tasks. Getting the help you need in these areas can mean the difference between growing your business to the next level or remaining stagnant.

Here are a few suggestions of different projects that can be delegated:

• Marketing projects: e-newsletters, press releases, social networking, database maintenance, appointment scheduling, business-to-business prospect calling, seminar assistance, seeking out and finding speaking engagements.

- Administrative tasks: Setting up of new clients, data entry, book-keeping, word processing, PowerPoint presentations, spreadsheets, Internet research, event planning and scheduling of travel or meal arrangements, just to name a few.

Where to Find a Virtual Assistant

You can research virtual assistants, either in your area or outside your area. There are several ways to find a VA:

- Get a referral from a business associate.

- Go to www.craigslist.com and look at the small business ads.

- Search Google® for a virtual assistant and/or personal assistant and look through virtual assistant directories.

There are many VA directories. It is best to use a virtual assistant service or an organization where they certify virtual assistants such as Assistu at www.assistu.com or the International Virtual Assistants Association (IVAA) at www.ivaa.org.

What to Look for in a Virtual Assistant

Whichever way you have chosen to look for your VA, you want to find someone who can complete your tasks professionally and on time. Make sure the VA has a business license. It helps if he or she is incorporated because this may relieve you from having to send a 1099 at the end of the year. It also might take out the guesswork as to whether or not the person qualifies as an independent contractor. Check www.irs.gov to see the independent contractor requirements.

Questions to Ask at the Interview

• For whom has the VA worked in the past? Obtain a list of testimonials.

• To what business groups and professional associations does he or she belong?

• What is the VA's specialty? Does it match with the list of projects you want to delegate? It is a benefit to use a VA who specializes in certain areas like customer support, Internet marketing support or speaker support. He or she will have in-depth knowledge and will be more experienced in the specialty area.

• How long has the individual been a VA?

• Ask for examples of work he or she has done. If that is not possible due to the type of project, ask how the VA did it and what steps were followed.

• Ask about work history. It can very important to know that he or she has worked in the corporate world at some time. This is the best training for a VA.

• What is the VA's turnaround time?

• What is his or her availability? Will you be able to contact this person when you need a question answered during your workday, or possibly after hours?

• What are his or her hobbies? You can learn a lot about people by just knowing what their hobbies are.

• What type of payments does the VA accept? Is he or she set up for credit cards?

• What does the VA charge?

Calling Business References

Once you know you are interested in hiring the virtual assistant, it is time to ask for four business references. Ask for names of people with or for whom the individual worked.

A few questions to ask are:

• What are (applicant's name) strengths?

• What are (applicant's name) weaknesses?

• How long have you known (applicant's name)?

• How long did you work with (applicant's name)?

Some companies can only verify the dates the employee worked with them, salary and title. However, for the most part, employers and/or co-workers are happy to answer your questions. Your conversation with them will give you great insight into the person you are considering.

What to Start Delegating

Now that you have picked the virtual assistant you feel will meet your needs, it's time to start delegating. First, start him or her off on a project that only you will see. If that goes well, you are happy with the work and you feel you really know this person, start sending your VA either harder projects and/or projects that involve your clients. Then you are on your way.

A virtual assistant can either make or break a business. I actually spoke to a business owner who had to change the name of his company because the VA he hired ruined his reputation. This is where it is really important that you know and trust your virtual assistant before you have him or her work on projects that involve your clients and/or prospects. By starting your VA off on easy projects first, you can see how this person operates and whether you are happy with the performance. It is key to know that the virtual assistant is professional and trustworthy.

You may need more than one virtual assistant to fit your needs. It depends on each VA's specialty. It is also to your advantage to have more than one virtual assistant so you will have a backup in case one of them is unavailable or gets sick.

The Art of Delegating

Here are a few suggestions on delegating effectively:

• To make delegating work, it takes good communication on both sides. It is important when you give your virtual assistant a project that you state when you want the project completed. If he or she is unable to complete the project by the deadline, the VA needs to let you know as soon as possible so you can make other arrangements by going to your backup VA.

• If the project you are delegating is part of a bigger project, it is important that the VA knows what the objective is. Knowing the big picture helps him or her complete the task correctly.

• Send all of your instructions via email. This way, your VA will be able to refer to them regularly. If your project will be done multiple times, enter the instructions in a Microsoft Word® document so you can resend it at a later time.

• Schedule a phone call with your VA after the project has been started. This way, if there are any questions, you will be available.

- Check in periodically via email to make sure the project is on track.

- Explain the task and then leave it up to the VA to get the project done. I like this quote from U.S. Army General George S. Patton: "Don't tell people how to do things, tell them what to do and let them surprise you with their ingenuity."

- Last, but not least, thank your VA for doing a great job. Make him or her feel appreciated.

To assist the workflow and further communication, you can utilize online tools that will help you and your VA access necessary, current information in a timely manner. There are many online tools that can help you delegate even more effectively and still have a handle on what is being done. Google has document sharing services where you and those you select can share documents and spreadsheets with real-time online access to the most current version. Accounting programs like Quickbooks® and Peachtree® offer online access that will allow your bookkeeping VA to make entries and process financial information from his or her location while you can access your information, run reports and know where you stand financially at any given moment.

By giving your VA honest feedback throughout the project, you will always be on the same page with him or her; ask the same of your VA. Most people appreciate honest, constructive feedback that will help them perform more efficiently at what they do. Provide this for your VA and you will build a good working relationship. When you first delve into the realm of using a VA, you will undoubtedly find areas you need to tweak and improve on to make delegating your workload work for you. Be open to feedback so you can learn how to better communicate and delegate.

Building the Team

It's important that everyone on the team get to know each other. While building your team, it is a good idea to evaluate the personalities to make sure everyone will be a good fit so they will work well together.

Schedule weekly meetings via a conference call. Talk about the big picture and what each team member's part will be for that week. This will create excitement, a sense of ownership and everyone will feel part of the team.

During the week, keep everyone in the loop through consistent communication. For example, include them in the appropriate company communications (e.g., e-newsletters, press releases, etc.). Share the accomplishments and milestones of your business and express appreciation for their involvement.

Appoint one person to be the team leader. This individual will over-see the projects and make sure the deadlines are met. This person will also create unity amongst the team members.

As you build and delegate, you are laying an even stronger foundation for your business. This will allow for greater customer satisfaction and continued growth. Make sure your foundation is firm!

Paying Your Virtual Assistant

Most virtual assistants bill once a month or upon completion of a project, whichever is first. You generally can pay by check or credit card, or even PayPal®. It depends on the arrangements you have made with your VA.

Ask your virtual assistant to submit invoices as close to the completion of work as possible, for example, by the third of the month for the previous month if they bill monthly, or within two to three days of completion of a project. This way, everything is fresh in both your minds if you need to go over any of the details on the invoice.

Request a spreadsheet showing the breakdown of what you are being billed for so you can accurately track the cost of the projects involved. The spreadsheet would give you the time that the work was done, the amount of time spent on the project and a description of the project. This way you will know that the project was completed within a reasonable time and that you are paying a fair price.

Enjoy Your New Life with Your Virtual Team

Now visualize your life with a virtual team. What does it look like? Will you be able to leave the office knowing that things are being taken care of? Maybe it is a life with less stress and more time to spend with your family and/or friends or to take up a hobby. Are you working *on* your business instead of in your business?

However you plan to use your virtual team, enjoy the growth you will experience both personally and in your business. Remember, *nothing is impossible when you delegate.*

JOANNE LANG
Founder and President
The Personal Assistant

Helping you bring in the business by providing marketing assistance and support

(916) 716-5800
joanne@thepersonalassistant.com
www.thepersonalassistant.com

Joanne founded The Personal Assistant in 2004 in order to provide professional administrative services and support to entrepreneurs, executives and busy professionals. Her strong organizational, time management and communication skills were gained through more than twenty years of experience. She is experienced as an executive administrative assistant, licensed insurance agent and notary public.

The clients of The Personal Assistant include small business owners with up to five employees. Though the team can help all industries, they have special knowledge in the financial planning, health and life insurance, public speaking, estate planning and real estate industries.

Joanne's passion is to help take her clients' businesses to the next level by providing marketing assistance and administrative support without the overhead of in-house staff. Joanne specializes in coordinating speaking engagements, business-to-business marketing and seminar assistance, making The Personal Assistant one of Roseville's most sought-after business resources.

Three Habits to Improve Workplace Productivity
By Karen Sladick

"Productivity is never an accident. It is always the result of a commitment to excellence, intelligent planning and focused effort."
—Paul J. Meyer, American author and
personal development industry leader

The American workplace has often been called a "rat race." Workers are known to do whatever it takes to get ahead and earn the prized promotion. If we stand back and view it from afar, working is in fact similar to a race. Runners who excel consistently train, work through the tough times, have a positive outlook and are committed to putting in the effort required to perform their best.

In the work environment, some workers will place well in the race because of their excellent organizational skills, strong productivity and high level of focus and energy. Other workers will perform poorly because of consistent disorganization, lack of productivity and inability to stay focused. What causes this apparent difference? Habits. Good habits versus bad habits. Fortunately, bad workplace habits can be replaced with good workplace habits. Here are some strategies you can implement to encourage good habits and discourage bad habits.

Habit #1: Eliminate Distractions

In order to improve productivity, you have to improve your focus. To improve your focus, you have to eliminate distractions. All the stacks, gadgets and clutter sitting on your desk are huge distractions. Worse, clutter is contagious! For example, have you ever sat at your desk, determined to work on a specific task, then moments later, find your attention shifting to a stack of work sitting on the corner of your desk? Did you stop working on the first task and start a new task from the other stack? By the end of the day, you have three or four partially completed tasks and a feeling of not having accomplished anything.

It may not seem like a big deal to toss a piece of paper in a stack on the corner of your desk, but stacks turn into piles, and piles turn into highly distracting, energy-draining, stress-producing clutter. When your desk is a mess, you are less likely to care if a few more items are tossed into the growing piles. If things are in order, you are more likely to keep them in order. When it comes to clutter, you need to sweat the small stuff. Small stuff turns into big stuff!

You might have tried to get rid of those stacks in the past, but for some reason, you abandoned the project before you had the chance to completely finish it. You had great intentions and got off to a great start, but the clutter eventually overwhelmed you, and you gave up. This may have happened because you did not understand there are different phases of getting organized, as well as a definite order. This may sound too simple, but you have to take an organized approach to becoming more organized. In turn, this process will increase your productivity.

There are five steps to take for eliminating clutter to become more focused, organized and productive.

1. Pick the area in your work environment that will make the biggest difference in your productivity. For example, let's start by clearing off your desk.

2. Gather all the stacks, papers and tasks on which you are currently working and put everything in one stack in the middle of your desk.

3. Work through the stack and eliminate everything you absolutely do not need in order to complete your work responsibilities.

4. Prioritize the remaining papers and tasks by placing the most important items on top and the least important items on the bottom. Use deadline dates to help determine the order.

5. Place the most important task on your desk and place the rest of the items by order of importance or deadline dates in a file labeled "Pending." When you finish the first task, go to your "Pending" file and pull out the next task. Continue this process until the items in your "Pending" file have been completed.

It is important to keep each step separate and do the tasks in the proper order. Putting your stacks in order of importance or by deadline dates must come before you start the first task. Do not get anxious and start working on a new task before you complete the current task. Stay focused, watch the clutter disappear, and see your productivity improve.

It is likely your stacks will grow again. Often, this happens at the start of a new week or month. No problem. Before you get overwhelmed, stop for a few minutes and go through the five steps mentioned above to get back on track. The good news is that you recognized you were heading down the path of clutter, disorganization and unproductive behavior and immediately interjected your new organizational habit. For more about office organization, see Nancy LaMont's chapter, *How to Have a Royally Organized Office,* on page 77.

Habit #2: Improve Your Focus

"When you're riding, only the race in which
you're riding is important."
—Bill Shoemaker, American jockey and winner of
eleven Triple Crowns

Because you have improved your ability to concentrate by eliminating the distractions in your workspace, we can now address another productivity improving habit: Maximizing your ability to focus.

Focusing and multi-tasking are not the same things. Focusing is thinking about the task or activity you are doing while you are engaged in it—one task or activity at a time. Focused concentration equates to high levels of productivity.

Unfortunately, we are often engaged in one task or activity while we are thinking about something else entirely. Sometimes, we are engaged in two or more tasks or activities at the same time and performing none of them as best we can. Multi-tasking equates to low levels of productivity.

When you are talking on the phone and typing an email, are you truly doing two things at the same time? No, it's impossible. Instead of engaging in two tasks at the same time, your mind is rapidly switching back and forth between both tasks. Neither task is receiving your full attention. Have you ever had to stop in the middle of your conversation and say, "I'm sorry, what was that you said?" If so, you were experiencing one of the negative effects of multi-tasking—not being effective at either task.

If you work in a hectic office and do not have the ability to close your door, or if you are a cubicle dweller, you probably multi-task more than you think you do. If you find you accomplished only a fraction of what you had planned to do at the end of the day, chances are you are allowing too many interruptions and distractions. If you work on a task that requires your attention and could be completed in thirty minutes with focused attention, is it more productive to keep working and finish the task or should you allow the interruption to pull you away from the task?

In a 2004 study by Dr. Gloria Mark, professor, Department of Informatics, University of California, Irvine, cubicle dwellers were observed for more than 1,000 hours. The study noted how many times employees were interrupted and how long each employee was able to work on any individual task. The results might surprise you:

- Each employee spent only 11 minutes on any given project before being interrupted and whisked off to do something else.

- Even worse, each eleven-minute project was, itself, fragmented into even shorter three-minute tasks, such as answering email, answering the phone or reading a web page.

- Each time a worker was distracted from a task, it would take an average of 25 minutes to return to that task. When the interruption was over, the office workers appeared to literally forget what task they were originally working on.

The biggest problem with interruptions is not really the interruptions at all. It's the havoc they wreak on our short-term memory. The next time you're focused and working on a task, and an email pops up or the phone rings, ask yourself, "How much more time do I need to finish the task at hand before allowing an interruption?" If it's thirty minutes or less, don't allow the interruption; let voicemail pick up or read the email or text message later. Finish your task and see how great you feel.

One more interesting observation from Dr. Mark's study—only 1 percent of the interruptions recorded represented actual emergencies; 99 percent of the interruptions could have been ignored when they occurred.

How can you leave the ineffective habit of multi-tasking behind while replacing it with the effective habit of focusing? Begin by consciously and deliberately practicing being in a focused state of mind. Professional athletes have capitalized on this practice for years. Let's discover what they do to achieve a focused state of mind.

When an athlete is preparing to compete, he or she usually performs a ritual or focuses on an identified cue. For example, every time a golfer steps up to the tee, he or she may take three practice swings and shrug a shoulder before making contact with the ball. A basketball player may bounce the ball two times and take a deep breath before shooting a foul shot. These rituals or cues get them focused on the task. It drowns out all the distractions around them.

The same concept applies to you in your workplace. Develop a ritual or a pre-determined cue to get your mind focused on what it is you need to do. Choose a ritual or a cueing device that reminds you of what you are going to be doing, instead of what you feel like doing. For example, a green, flat marble sits on my desk. Every time I sit down to work on a task that requires my focus, I look at the marble (my cueing device) and remind myself that "right now" I need to focus on the task. The marble reminds me to ignore email and let the phone calls go to voicemail. I stay focused on the task. The more you deliberately practice this focusing technique, the better your habits and your productivity will be.

Sometimes, just getting started on the task is the hardest part. Once you take action, you become energized and it makes it harder to stop. Since it is hard to focus to begin with, eliminating distractions is a core skill for staying focused. Turn everything off when you have decided that it is time to focus.

As much as focusing on one task at a time is highly productive, multi-tasking is sometimes unavoidable. That's life. However, you will need to be determined to honor those times when focusing would be more productive. In fact, you only have to recognize this 20 percent of the time.

Habit #3: Reap Results from the Pareto Principle

In general, it appears that the majority of our results come from the minority of our efforts. This is often referred to as the Pareto Principle or the 80/20 Rule. There is no particular magic to the numbers "80" and "20." These numbers were simply chosen to represent the relationship of imbalance that exists between our efforts and results.

Vilfredo Pareto, an Italian economist and sociologist, coined the term "80/20 Rule" in 1906 when he noticed roughly 80 percent of the wealth in developed economies seemed to end up in the hands of 20 percent of the people. Other prominent observers later expanded on Pareto's findings and concluded that his principle applied to many areas of life.

Most people understand the implications of the Pareto Principle. However, many people think of the implications in the same way they think of car accidents, natural disasters, crime and so on. They think these things primarily happen to other people, or in the case of the Pareto Principle, apply to other people. The Pareto Principle is the solution to not having enough time or to being overloaded. Ironically, many people cannot see it.

To put things in perspective, we need to reword Pareto's idea: Eighty percent of what you are doing probably does not matter! This idea is important.

How can this translate into improving your workday? If 80 percent of your results come from 20 percent of your efforts, it would make sense to practice being highly focused for 20 percent of your day. Assuming you work an 8-hour day, 20 percent of an 8-hour day is 96 minutes. If you can practice being focused for 96 minutes each day, you will accomplish 80 percent of what you need to do. Doesn't that sound great?

Invest in a timer and set it for 96 minutes. While the timer is running, turn off your email alerts, let your phone go to voicemail and focus on the task.

Let the Pareto Principle, the 80/20 Rule, serve as a daily reminder to focus your time and energy on your most important work. Do not just "work smart," work smart on the things that matter.

Focus takes energy. Every time you focus on a task, you utilize some of your limited supply of attention. You can only stay focused for so long before the work starts to drain you. Each task you do tends to make you less effective at the next task.

This is especially true for tasks that are high energy, like making decisions and handling uncomfortable situations. Since most of us are more effective and have more energy in the morning than in the afternoon, tackle those high-energy tasks as early in the day as possible. Other obligations can sometimes eat up your morning time, but if time allows, do the high-energy tasks first.

"Excellence is an art won by training and habituation. We do not act rightly because we have virtue or excellence, but we rather have those because we have acted rightly. We are what we repeatedly do. Excellence, then, is not an act but a habit."
—Aristotle, Greek philosopher

How can you be excellent in your workplace? Think about runners training for a race. Every day they train in some way. It is a habit they perform because they desire certain results.

You can train by organizing your workspace, eliminating the distractions around you and working effectively for short periods. These strategies will increase your productivity and decrease your stress. You will place well in the race because you possess excellent organizational skills and high levels of focus, energy and productivity. Your good habits will cause you to sail across the finish line, well ahead of the pack. Have a positively productive day!

KAREN SLADICK
Organize 4 Results

Helping businesses become more organized, focused and productive

(205) 907-5170
karen@organize4results.com
www.organize4results.com

Karen Sladick founded Organize 4 Results in 2007. She specializes in conducting seminars for businesses to help employees increase organizational skills and become more focused and productive in the workplace. Her extensive research and study of the mental and physical aspects of organization provide seminar participants with simple, specific and effective solutions to workplace stress. These solutions help participants ensure quality, productive work time; decrease productivity-killing stress and anxiety; improve the ability to follow through on projects and recover quickly from interruptions.

Teaching organizational techniques in an entertaining, high-energy style, Karen motivates participants to implement the techniques into their everyday lives. They discover her techniques significantly improve workplace results.

Karen works with clients in a variety of professional settings and is certified to teach continuing education courses for the Alabama Real Estate Commission, Alabama Board of Nursing, Alabama and Georgia State Bar, Alabama Board of Public Accountancy, Tennessee Commission on Continuing Legal Education and the State of Mississippi Judiciary. She is the author of *Tools for a Successful Closing,* an approved course for the Alabama Real Estate Commission. She is also the co-author of *Success Skills for Life*™, the organization and etiquette guide that prepares students for success in life. She is a graduate of Michigan State University.

Your Perfect First and Every Impression for Success

You Are Your Most Powerful Marketing Tool!

By Mary Kot, AICI FLC

"Like it or not, it is that first impression which will dictate future associations—more than performance, more than family, and more than all the time and effort you have spent to be both well-educated and adequate in your chosen profession...Your credibility and, chances are, your lifelong...niche were just established by the first impression you made through your appearance."
—William Thourlby, American author

*A*n incredible first impression—and every impression you present to your business clients and colleagues—will empower you to maximize the talents with which you have been blessed. It can:

• Spark greater success for you.

• Communicate you are dependable, organized, capable and competent.

• Distinguish you from your peers.

• Position you for promotion.

• Energize you.

• Give you additional power to persuade and influence others.

• Most importantly, give you the confidence to achieve your goals and desires.

For an incredible business impression, make your first and every impression work for you. Each time you encounter people, they judge you based on your appearance, body language and speech. They will assess your credibility, honesty, competency and likeability based on the clothing you wear, your hairstyle, your grooming, the way you speak and the types of body language and facial expressions you project. You can make these judgments work in your favor. You have the ability to choose how you appear and the attitude you project to others: powerful, competent, confident, positive, energetic, likeable or successful.

A friend and colleague had to be convinced that her appearance negatively affected her performance on the board of directors of a nonprofit corporation. As one of the leading experts in her field, she was discouraged and frustrated with the lack of influence she was able to wield on this board. Her appearance was insignificant to her. She was highly educated, an authority in her area of expertise and she firmly believed this should be enough to command respect from her fellow board members. It was not.

Eventually, with my coaching, she agreed to an image makeover. After coloring, cutting and styling her hair, teaching her to apply makeup and convincing her to wear a jacket to all board meetings, her transformation was complete. She now had an incredible business image and she embraced it. Within a year, not only was she able to convince and persuade her colleagues to consider her point of view, she was elected president of the board of directors, an accomplishment she could not have envisioned prior to her image makeover. She is a perfect illustration of the value of a positive incredible first impression during every business encounter.

Maximize Your Most Influential Marketing Tool

You are your most influential marketing tool. To take full advantage of this powerful instrument, planning and preparation are critical. How many opportunities will you have to make a powerful impression when it really counts? How often are you in front of a decision maker who can change the course of your future success? Now is the time to prepare for the next promotion or business opportunity that may arise or for the sales meeting that will land you the contract of your dreams.

Begin immediately to prepare and plan the first impression you need to gain an advantage over your competition and to position yourself for ultimate business success. Make an honest assessment of your personal assets and your weaknesses. Ask friends and family members for feedback to obtain an accurate analysis of how you are currently perceived by others. Consider a consultation with an image consultant.

Listed below are factors influencing the impression you present to others. Evaluate your interpersonal skills, body language, appearance, speech and manners. Analyze the areas you want to improve and list them in priority order.

Master Your Body Language to Work to Your Advantage

You control your body language. Body language includes attitude, posture, body movement and facial expression. The impression you make when meeting new associates or prospective customers will be greatly enhanced by using the proper handshake and eye contact. Turn your body to face the person, smile and maintain eye contact while fully extending your right hand, and, with a firm grip, pump the person's hand two or three times. To help you remember the person's name, repeat it as you shake hands and as you tell him or her how pleased you are to make his or her acquaintance.

Adopt body language that will create rapport with others. To increase your likeability factor, smile easily and often. A ready, friendly smile will compel others to smile back. Smiling is contagious. Science shows us that smiling sets off a chemical reaction in the brain that increases our endorphin level, creating a natural high. Try it when you need a lift. You can practice smiling at yourself in a mirror. You will feel better.

Project positive energy to maximize your business impression. A colleague of mine consistently draws a crowd at networking events because of his happy and optimistic attitude. He always has an interesting anecdote or story to relate, and he projects a relaxed and friendly energy. If you are not naturally optimistic, you can teach yourself to be. Focus daily on your successes and tell yourself you can accomplish the goals you have set for yourself. A confident, positive attitude and energy are good for business.

How would you describe your posture? Stand against a wall in your normal stance. Are your shoulder blades touching the wall? Would you describe your posture as erect with shoulders back, indicating confidence, or do you have a slightly hunched posture, possibly suggesting defeat or rejection? Maybe your shoulders are in a permanently raised position, signifying discomfort, or are retracted and tense, portraying anger or a sense of superiority.

You can immediately improve your visual image by standing tall and stretching your neck upwards, as if a string were pulling up on your head. Roll your shoulders up, back and down, and bring them to rest in a relaxed position. Squeeze your stomach muscles in and pull your navel toward your spine. Be aware of your posture so you can control what you are projecting to others.

Your Body Movement Indicates Mood

Your body movements communicate important information to your business associates. How you move when walking, sitting down, getting up, the body movements you make while talking, listening, even breathing, signal your mood. Successful business professionals, like actors or poker players, control their body language to telegraph the information they want to communicate.

Youthful vitality is prized in our competitive business market. To convey a youthful energy, walk with a purposeful, confident stride with your head up, looking straight ahead. Walking slowly with a stiff gait projects tiredness, just as collapsing into your seat or rising in a halting manner from your chair indicates a lack of energy. The perception of energy and vitality is an immense benefit in the business world.

Facial expressions signal our moods. Cues about the moods of our co-workers are obtained mainly from facial expressions. Be aware of the facial expression you wear as you go about your day. Others will be drawn to pleasant facial expressions and repelled by angry or unfriendly ones. Maintain an amicable facial expression to garner more favorable responses from others.

People Make Instant Judgments

Within minutes of meeting or interviewing you, business professionals will determine whether they will hire you or do business with you based on your body language, appearance and speaking skills. You may be able to alter the first impression that you present, but if you can assure success by creating an incredible first impression at the start, why not do so?

Begin with your wardrobe. High-quality clothing that fits well, in a current style, appropriate for the industry and the occasion will promote a strong, positive impression. Quality accessories—such as shoes, a handbag or a briefcase—will reinforce your positive impression. Jewelry should be kept to a minimum.

Daily good grooming habits are essential in generating a favorable impression. So too, are clean, neatly filed nails, a current hairstyle and fashionable eyewear. Eyebrows for men and women are best when neatly trimmed and groomed. However, beware of over-plucked brows. They may age you beyond your years. Makeup for women is encouraged. Women who wear makeup are viewed as more credible and competent. A clean-shaven face is best for men in the business world. Facial hair will detract from your business image.

Consider your level of professional credibility. To project your most incredible business image you will need to be perceived as reliable, honest, hard-working, sincere, competent, capable and energetic. This list may sound daunting, but if you commit to always doing your best, exceeding expectations when possible, and treating co-workers and associates with kindness and respect, you will have succeeded in establishing excellent professional credibility.

Encourage respect by cultivating your speaking and listening skills. Listen carefully to what business associates and coworkers are telling you. Take a genuine interest in their concerns and problems. They will reciprocate. You will both benefit, and your communication skills and effectiveness will grow. For more information on the value of listening, see page 149 for Suzanne Zazulak Pedro's chapter *Beyond the Art of Listening.*

Gain extra authority when speaking to business associates by using proper grammar and avoiding unnecessary, controversial subjects and bad language. Display your confidence and competence when speaking, by eliminating "up-talking"—making the last word of a statement sound as if you are asking a question. Lend additional credibility to your business image by speaking clearly and enunciating each word.

Enhance and manage your electronic impression by carefully proofreading your email communications to ensure all words are fully spelled out, that you have used complete sentences, and that your grammar is correct. Safeguard your business reputation by sending only emails you would be comfortable having any business associate read, and refrain from sending angry emails.

Aligning the image on your social networking sites to the business image you have chosen to convey is recommended. One day, your business associates may very well end up viewing these sites with or without your permission. A professional email address will substantiate your business image while a frivolous one such as "crazyJoe@Joe.com" will detract from it. For more information on your online impression, see the chapter *Online Social Networking for Business* by Karen Clark on page 213 in this book.

Business Meetings: An Opportunity to Achieve an Incredible Impression

Imagine you are scheduled to participate in a large business meeting with a group of twenty or more people. This is the perfect opportunity to showcase the new image you have created for yourself.

Arrive five to ten minutes before the start of the meeting to ensure that you are on time and not rushed. If you have just finished lunch and are refreshing your breath with chewing gum, now would be the time to dispense with it. Smacking and popping gum in a meeting is not considered professional and can annoy others.

Enter the room with calm, confident poise. Carry a slim leather briefcase or leather notepad with a nice pen. Women may want to consider carrying their wallets in a briefcase. Briefcases look more professional than purses. Avoid being weighed down with books and file folders. Successful executives do not lug around a lot of files and papers. As an aside, if you bring your lunch to work, place it in your briefcase for a more professional appearance on your way to work.

It is perfectly fine to check your emails until the start of the meeting, but turn off the ringer on your cell phone. After the meeting begins, scrolling through your email, texting or doodling implies you are bored. You may well be bored, but I would encourage you not to show it. Your best impression will be secured by appearing interested and engaged.

If you use reading glasses, be mindful of how you peer over them or through them. During a meeting, it is not uncommon to see professionals contorting their faces in a strange manner to see around and above their reading glasses. For maximum credibility, check yourself in a mirror at home to avoid creating odd expressions when you look up at someone while wearing your reading glasses. This situation may be avoided by purchasing progressive lenses or wearing a contact lens in one eye for reading.

Your personal presence will be most enhanced by sitting up straight in your chair and maintaining your best posture. Rocking or tilting your chair may result in an embarrassing backwards flip. Tapping your foot or your pen or making any other similar, repetitive motion will negatively impact your business impression. If you have a repetitive habit, such as shaking your leg or twiddling your thumbs, once you are aware of it, you can work to eliminate it. You may want to consult with a friend and ask if you unconsciously exhibit any of these habits.

If you are not feeling well, it can be challenging to project your most powerful business impression. Try to minimize the impact of your illness. If you are suffering from a severe head cold or allergy and need to blow your nose during the meeting, excuse yourself and go to the restroom. Loud nose blowing can be very distracting to others and will not enhance your credibility.

Notice the facial expressions of those in the room. Be aware of your own facial mask—the expression on your face in repose. Often while listening, the facial masks that appear on participants' faces are not flattering. Determine if your facial mask is portraying the expression you want to communicate. Be aware of your facial mask and focus on making some adjustments if necessary. This is another opportunity to watch yourself and observe your expressions while you are on the telephone.

Commit to Capitalizing on Your Assets

"…There is one simple thing that you can alter and thereby dramatically change your life. You can change your appearance, by packaging yourself to achieve specific goals, and become happier, successful and even richer."

—William Thourlby, American author

Maximize your most powerful marketing tool—yourself. Launch the new image you will need to accomplish your dreams. Visualize yourself interacting with your coworkers and business associates while projecting the image you have created for yourself. The more often you envision yourself as a poised, positive, competent and confident professional, the more quickly your transformation to your new business image will occur.

Devise the strategy you will need to transform yourself. Capitalize on your strengths. Improve on your shortcomings. Align your visual image with your inner self. Prepare now for the role you want in life and dress the part.

Document what you need to focus on to obtain this image. Set goals for yourself and a date to accomplish each goal. Immediately begin to incorporate new strategies into your daily grooming and dressing routine. A gradual integration of the modifications and additions to establish your new image will ensure that each change feels natural and comfortable to you.

Once your transformation is complete, your first impression and every impression will project an incredible business image and will guide others to clearly see your capabilities and attributes. You will be more persuasive and influential, and you will be poised to maximize your most influential marketing tool—yourself. You will have an advantage over your competition, and distinguish yourself from your peers. You will communicate to all that you are prepared for any challenge, and you will gain the confidence to meet those challenges.

MARY KOT, AICI FLC
Executive Impressions

Helping you make the perfect impression

(610) 952-5225
mary@execimpressions.com
www.execimpressions.com

Mary is the founder and owner of Executive Impressions, an image consulting firm that specializes in image management for individuals and businesses. Consulting services and workshops are offered in all facets of image consulting, including empowerment through image, anti-aging techniques, body language, custom color analysis, body style analysis and virtual body style analysis.

Executive Impressions works with business professionals who are often feeling frustrated with their level of success. By enhancing their strengths and improving areas of vulnerability through individualized image management strategies, clients gain confidence and a more powerful and professional image, resulting in greater personal fulfillment and success.

Mary is a former accountant with a bachelor's degree in business administration. Mary gave up accounting to follow her passion of helping others feel more confident about their appearance and perfect their image for success. An advisor to many successful political campaigns and an active community member, Mary serves on several nonprofit boards in her hometown of West Chester, Pennsylvania, and is Vice President of Education and Secretary for the Association of Image Consultants International, Ohio-Pennsylvania Chapter. Mary received her image consulting certification at the renowned Stoltz Image Institute, under the direction of Elaine Stoltz, AICI CIM.

How to Create Impact with Your Own True Class Act

By Tiffany Nielsen

*W*hen I was a young girl, my father taught me that if you make an agreement with another person, you honor it. Looking back, I can see how lucky I was to have received this early lesson in becoming a true class act in the business world. I am grateful to learn more every day about how the outward show of professionalism allows us to transcend all sorts of boundaries.

No matter where you are in your own life, you are presented with endless opportunities to build rapport and trust with people from many cultures, industries and experiences. Acting professionally does not mean losing your personality or being forced to live in a box. Conducting business in an ethical, considerate, joyful manner is an individual choice with potential for huge impact on building all sorts of incredible business!

Developing an outstanding professional reputation and an image with impact takes commitment, practice and a willingness to make some mistakes along the way. I have made my fair share of blunders and *faux pas* but they taught me and helped make me a respected leader in my industry today.

My first job out of college found me on the receiving end of an angry lecture from my boss. He caught me with my feet up on my desk while I was talking to a friend on the phone. This experience helped me recognize that genuine professional success is built upon self-respect, and it has helped me find purpose in guiding you to develop your own unique professional image. By the way, your image is more than just your appearance—communication and behavior are also key elements. The following tips can help you create impact with your own true class act.

Start Your Day Right

Recognize that it is your responsibility to set yourself up right to have a great day. This starts with a good night's sleep, a healthy breakfast and the right attitude. Greet yourself in the mirror with a hearty, "Good morning, Superstar!"

Consider your own best tips for health and happiness. Prepare a list and post it on your bathroom mirror to serve as a daily reminder of what will help you feel thoroughly prepared to shine. Some items to consider: drink water, take vitamins, get some exercise, be grateful and kiss your spouse or partner.

Plan Your Dress, Dress Your Plan

> *"Know yourself first, and then adorn yourself accordingly."*
> —Epictetus, Greek philosopher

When you look great, it sends a message that you are professional, confident and competent. Your client's confidence in you starts with your appearance. To look great everyday, start your day out right the night before. Before you go to bed, lay out your clothes for the next day. When selecting your garments, be thoughtful of the people and circumstances you will be addressing. Make sure your clothes are clean, pressed and need no repair. This can save you a ton of time and aggravation in the morning.

In the workplace, there is lots of talk about dress code policies. It isn't so much about policy, but about your complementing yourself and your surroundings. Ask yourself what image will project the right message about your work. Each of us has a certain style. Successfully build your personal impact into your wardrobe without breaking company policy. A professional image draws attention to your eyes and face and makes people want to listen to your message. Buy clothes that fit well, enhance your body's positives and conceal your shape challenges.

Get clear on color. Heed the advice of my favorite French designer, Coco Chanel: "The best color in the whole world is the one that looks good on you!" There are many colors you can wear that will complement your image. Stand in front of a well-lit mirror and place different colored shirts, scarves or swatches near your face to see which colors brighten or dull your complexion. A number of colors will fit your image perfectly. For extra help, consider hiring an image consultant who can show you what colors highlight your best features. This small investment will save you many times over in avoiding colors that do not look good on you.

In addition to learning what colors are best for you, invest time in organizing your closet. Start by separating your career clothes from your formal, cocktail and casual wear. Use this time also to remove and donate outfits that are no longer appropriate to your image. Whether traveling to several business meetings in one day, delivering a presentation to a client or working from your office, you can more efficiently discover the perfect outfit that will work for each project if your closet is well-organized. Looking as good in the evening as you did in the morning calls for a "one-outfit-that-suits-all" approach. Here are some useful guidelines to keep you looking great all day:

• Be comfortable and dress to impress your clients. Inquire about their workplace dress codes before you meet them.

• To be extra successful with your appearance, dress up a bit more than what is expected. Your attention to this detail will let others notice you as someone they can take seriously with their business.

• For a day full of multiple meetings and presentations, choose a suit that can be dressed up and down in a matter of seconds. Men, to stand out without sticking out when moving from formal to casual business mode, remove your tie, jacket or both depending upon the client. Ladies, a simple black, tailored dress is an essential wardrobe piece for you. You can suit up a tailored black dress by adding a sophisticated jacket and closed-toe pumps. You can transform this same dress to a business casual look by wearing a sweater that buttons in the front and changing out your heels for dressy, but conservative, flat shoes. Add a shawl and dressy jewelry, and it becomes very easy for you to go from work to an evening affair.

• Jeans may work for a casual look in your office or that of a client. Choose dark blue or black denim jeans that fit your body type and are not too tight or low on the hips. The best fit is one that flatters your body and still looks professional.

Focusing attention on your image has a favorable impact on your own self-confidence and sets a strong foundation for your business.

Be on Time

To earn the respect of others, you have to honor your commitments or have reasons and solutions when you cannot. As an etiquette speaker and trainer, one of the most frequent complaints I hear from my clients is about people being late to meetings and appointments. If you find yourself in a situation where you will not be on time, never wait until the last minute to take action. People would rather you be honest than be a no-show or arrive with nothing to offer but excuses. It is important to your credibility to give plenty of notice, apologize and make a new commitment (if possible and permitted). By arriving on time, you demonstrate professionalism and become a role model of how others should treat you in return.

Go Beyond the Expected

Be service-minded. If you want to conduct impactful business, ask yourself what you can offer above and beyond what is expected of you by clients, employers, partners and other associates. Strive to make their jobs easier by bringing more value to their business. For example:

• Offer discounts or give away free products or services.

• Make a donation to their favorite charity.

• Offer free seminars/trainings.

• Answer questions promptly and follow through on assignments.

• Remember birthdays!

• Know the expectations of your bosses and clients and present solutions good for the client, not just you.

• Be organized.

What can you do to exceed expectations?

Dazzle people! Get them to say, "Wow, you've put in a lot of work here!" Some examples that can set you apart from your competition are staying late to finish an assignment, helping a colleague or client who is struggling to meet a deadline, arriving early at meetings, sending a handwritten thank you card to people who helped you achieve a task, or recommending a person who meets or exceeds your expectations.

Trust that when you go beyond the expected and serve others, your efforts will be recognized. The rewards can be lasting and profitable business relationships.

Be a Problem Solver

Everyone makes mistakes. There is nothing more uplifting you can do for others than to own up to a problem you have created and offer solutions that are best for everyone rather than just yourself. If roles are reversed, be as considerate as possible to someone who has made a mistake. Encourage others to find inner strength to practice honesty, humility and kindness.

The most difficult problems are caused by those who refuse the opportunity to learn from mistakes. You may not be in a position to point out the mistakes of others, but you can positively impact your business by showing your willingness to learn from your mistakes. Problems are best solved in an atmosphere of mutual trust that builds long-term, profitable business relationships.

Respect Your Reputation

You can remain professional and still have a good time at any event. On the other hand, a careless attitude can lead to trouble. Having fun at company gatherings is a must. Why else would they be organized in the first place? They are meant to help people grow closer to each other for the good of the business.

Here are some tips for having fun and staying professional:

• Dressing well for company parties will put you at ease. If you are unsure of the dress code, ask the person in charge of the event for guidelines. If you are the host, mention the dress code in the announcement.

- If you drink alcohol, enjoy what is offered but limit your intake.

- Encourage positive conversation. Speak about how much you appreciate being at the event and what you like about the location, food and people who are sharing the good time with you. You may also have fun sharing thoughts on current events, movies, entertainment, families and travel. Refraining from discussions related to politics and religion is smart unless it directly relates to the success and nature of your business.

- If you are the host, warmly welcome your guests. If you are the guest, sincerely thank the host (business owner, manager and event planner) for inviting you to the event. Expressing gratitude in person shows your sincere character. A handwritten thank-you note will impress even more.

- When you are attending sporting events with clients and colleagues, be the person who encourages sportsmanship. Cheer on the visiting team as well as the home team. This kind of behavior will influence your company to see you as a business leader who encourages fairness and respect.

- Golf remains one of the most common forms of business entertainment. If you are not a golfer and your clients want to play, consider taking a few golf lessons before tee-time and reading tips on golf etiquette. This will considerably raise your confidence while furthering your business relationships.

Company events provide you the perfect opportunity to be a good example to others. Your good manners and common sense will attract others and cement your reputation as a truly friendly class act in the business world.

Observe and Maintain Professional Protocols

I encourage every business, group and individual with whom I work to establish a benchmark for business manners. Discuss and implement protocols that encourage respect and consideration for others. We all have a tendency to notice flaws in others that we have not yet recognized in ourselves.

• Ask permission before entering someone else's office or cubicle space.

• Answer the telephone before the third ring.

• Smile on the phone and in person.

• Turn off your cell phone or turn it to silent mode in meetings.

Of course, you want to avoid office gossip at all costs because it breeds negativity and hurt feelings. Instead, learn how to make small talk when appropriate to get to know others better. This is your best method for allowing yourself to build deeper relationships with colleagues and clients without speaking about overly personal subjects.

Here are three questions that may jump-start your conversation: What is the latest good news in your business? What exciting projects are you working on? What are you looking forward to doing next?

Dine with Impact

When dining with clients and colleagues, it is important to maintain your professional image. Etiquette at the table is serious business; many people will judge you by your table manners.

Business dining is meant to be relaxing for you and your guests. You will find that polishing your etiquette skills will help you enjoy being with your guests and engaging in any business that needs to be discussed.

American business dining etiquette tips are plentiful. Use these simple tips to help you improve your table manners quickly:

- If you are unsure of which utensil to use, look around to see which utensil your host(s) is using.

- Clients deserve the best seat in the house. Encourage them to choose the seat that will put their back to the wall. When making a reservation, politely request a table away from the bathroom and the wait station. This helps to avoid any unnecessary distraction and will likely land you one of the better tables in the restaurant.

- Rather than email a request, phone your clients to invite them out for a meal. Offer a choice of restaurants in your price range.

- Business over breakfast and lunch is best discussed after the order has been taken. Dinner is different. Practice relationship building by putting your best small talk skills to work before and during the entrée. Small general discussions about business are good up to that point, but heavier business-related discussions are best left until after the entrée is finished.

- Tip the wait staff well. It is customary to tip fifteen to twenty percent of the food bill. Tip this amount even if the service was not to your liking.

Learn the tenets of business dining etiquette so well that they become second nature, and you can concentrate with confidence on the business at hand. A gracious host or guest encourages others to feel comfortable and engage in easy conversation. Conducting business over a meal will never go out of style. An investment in upgrading your dining skills is of great benefit to making a good impression.

Be Fiscally Savvy

The smartest businessperson I know taught me to pay attention to my fiscal impact on my business associates, whether client or employer. Be respectful of how you use your time and the resources of your business—from not wasting your time on the job, to purchasing office supplies and minding your travel expenses. You always have the perfect opportunity to show that you are conscious of the bottom line and considerate of the resources available to you. This will always be appreciated and keep you on the job.

Additionally, always be looking for ways to save your clients or employer money. One of my clients, Jennifer, owned an advertising company and produced marketing collateral for mid-size companies. She frequently showed her clients ways that would save them money on their printing. As a result, they often raved about her and were very loyal.

Also, practice careful use of your own money. This will not only help you develop a greater respect for your own accomplishments, but further your business relationships with others who are serious about their financial well-being. The more money you make, the more you might be tempted to spend. However, it makes better business sense to spend more time making money than spending it! Spend what you must to increase your professional skills while saving something for a rainy day.

Be thrifty. Money demands respect if it is to become a strong, fruitful part of your business.

Keep it Simple

*"Always bear in mind that your own resolution to succeed
is more important than any other."*
—Abraham Lincoln, sixteenth president of the United States

Establishing your personal brand of professional conduct will attract a following of loyal customers.

Create one goal from each category above to help you strengthen your professional image.

As you develop your skills, begin to observe how approachable, dependable and confident you become. Our world needs more people like you: people who respect themselves enough to step up and out of the norm, enhance their image, demonstrate good business practices and achieve personal success. Become the person you aspire to be and watch your business thrive.

TIFFANY NIELSEN
Certified Etiquette Expert
and Image Consultant

(559) 280-9859
tiffany@tiffanynielsen.com
www.tiffanynielsen.com

Tiffany is founder and president of Premier Etiquette Training and Consulting, located in Exeter, California. She is a trained etiquette and image professional with expertise in professional development.

Tiffany served fifteen years in corporate management, overseeing and prospecting business development opportunities for large and small businesses before launching her etiquette and image speaking career in 2006. In addition to speaking, she delivers action-oriented, interactive seminars and private coaching sessions to small and large businesses, associations and young professionals. Her encouragement of the fine art of good manners in personal and business life is contagious and memorable.

A weekly business etiquette columnist for *Business Street Online,* Tiffany is the founder of the Etiquette Ambassador Youth Program™ and an avid volunteer in her community. She was selected Business Leader by *Business Street Online* in 2009 and voted most influential in her industry by *Forty Under Forty Most Influential.*

Tiffany holds a bachelor of science degree in agriculture business management from California Polytechnic State University, San Luis Obispo, California. She is a graduate of Dale Carnegie and was trained by the Emily Post Institute.

From Not to Hot!
Creating Sensational Customer Service Inside and Out
By Victoria Ashford

"Quality in a product or service is not what the supplier puts in. It is what the customer gets out and is willing to pay for. Customers pay only for what is of use to them and gives them value."
—Peter Drucker, Austrian author, management consultant

I get around in my daily life as a speaker, trainer and coach; I dine out, travel, shop and enjoy the benefits of an active lifestyle. I interact with a variety of people and experience a myriad of business practices—some are exemplary and desirable; some are not. This often gets me thinking about customer service.

Pick up most organizations' advertisements and promotional materials, watch their commercials, review their websites, amble through their corridors, or visit employees' cubicles, and it will be there—some statement, caption, plaque or award describing a commitment to customer service. What does customer service really mean, however? How is it attained and sustained in superlative form? Whose responsibility is it?

Over the years, I have developed an innovative formula—a model, really—that creates effective change and brings great results such as: increased sales or usage, great PR, cooperation and teamwork, additional revenue and employee retention, to name a few. If these outcomes appeal to you, this chapter will show you how my method can give you practical, proven tools to help you improve customer service, regardless of your business sector or industry.

Terms of Endearment

Before I reveal my blueprint, let's define a few key terms, starting with the obvious one—"customer service."

Customer service is all about *value,* about your customer being valued and feeling important. Who is your customer? If you immediately answered that it is the person or groups of people who utilize or purchase your goods and services, you are only partially correct. In my model, that response is a description of one type of customer's behavior.

More definitively, a customer is the internal or external person who has a present or future interest in your organization and whom you consistently value and deem important through attitude and actions. Notice the use of the words *internal* and *external.*

• **Internal Customers (ICs).** From the "inside out," also known as personnel, colleagues, co-workers, peers, staff, employees, board members, volunteers, cast, crew and so on.

• **External Customers (ECs).** From the "outside in," commonly identified as customers, guests, patrons, visitors or purchasers.

See the difference? Imagine what a wondrous and empowering business you will have when both groups are acknowledged and valued.

Look at your definition and change it to one that is more precise and inclusive. Write it down.

The Sensational Customer Service Formula

The formula for delivering sensational customer service is:

$$P^3 + C^3 = SCS!^{TM}$$

It looks like a complex mathematical equation, but it is really a simple—yet not simplistic—system to ensure your customers' needs are met, expectations are exceeded, and exceptional service is rendered. It stands for: P3 (Presentation, Personality, Programming) plus C3 (Care, Connection, Customization) equals SCS! (Sensational Customer Service!). Let's look at each part of the formula:

• **Presentation—the "how you look" component.** I like to enter cooking contests. I once entered a big one and came in second. Afterward, one of the judges told me my dessert was better than the winner's entrée. "What! Then how come I didn't win?" I asked disappointedly. "Presentation," the judge explained. He said the winner's food was average, but his presentation was significantly better. The judge was right—my competitor's display was awesome. He was a master food stylist and had appealed to the judges' eyes long before morsels ever went into their mouths. I learned the hard way that presentation can influence others' recognition and behavior.

The same phenomenon works in business. ICs and ECs are turned on or off by what they see about you, your work force, your furnishings, facilities and products. I encourage you to spend some time and money examining the visual aesthetic—eye appeal—of your business.

Not your strength or don't know where to start? Get the help of experts. Hire an image consultant, landscape architect, civil engineer or other design professional who will review your current impression and help you repair, upgrade or update it.

Remember my contest experience and improve your image. It will increase your influence and allow interested parties to see what you have to offer long before they seek employment or make a purchase.

- **Personality—the "who you are" component.** Most every living, breathing, animated creature has a personality; temperament traits may be labeled as "sparkly," "friendly," "helpful," and so on. Your business is no different.

Describe your organization in ten words or less.

Would ICs and ECs agree with you? If not, you may need to make some adjustments if your perception and reality do not match. One associate I know, who within a few weeks of being hired, was informed by her board president that their organization was known as "The Happy Library," and they wanted it to stay that way. At that moment, the new director had a keen awareness of the organization's personality—and its importance. Take the time to make your business' personality shine.

- **Programming—the "what you do or provide" component.** The question "What have you done for me lately?" is always lingering in the minds of your customers. Do you know how they would like that question answered? Utilizing suggestion boxes, online or mail-in surveys and other feedback instruments can inform you of what is happening within your business, and how it affects those outside it. Ignorance in this area is *not* bliss, and can cost you in the end.

It is sad to say, but ECs usually receive the lion's share of attention with regard to programming, where businesses are always trying to better their best practices. I ask you to turn your attention to your ICs for a moment with an action that is sure to astonish them. Learn and do part of their jobs on occasion. You will be amazed and instantly alerted to the effectiveness and efficiency of certain duties and disciplines.

When working with a company to improve their customer service, I find it enlightening to work in various departments. What I have discovered are some silly, redundant, time-wasting, long-term procedures. When I questioned others as to why these activities were being done, the response was usually, "We don't know; we've always done it like that."

When you do this and discover similar activities, you now have a great opportunity to eliminate fruitless behaviors and build a foundation for the next two elements.

• **Care—the "how you make them feel" component.** Embedded in every interaction or transaction is the question "Who am I to you?" Both ICs and ECs want to know this with certainty.

Here are some great ideas: Find out what matters most to those individuals or groups by becoming a careful observer. Learn how to vary your preferred communication and interaction styles to meet their preferences and needs. Systematically analyzing your practices will tell you if your approach is nurturing the kind of feelings you want.

One of the ways I have clients implement this component is through "wonder-working words." These phrases, sentences and questions convey heart or affect others positively. For example, use: *Yes; I'm sorry; I was wrong; Will you..., while I...?; Excellent; Well done; That's perfect; Any questions, comments or concerns?* Use these words liberally—or compose your own. They will work wonders. Another method I recommend is my three shows strategy.

Here is how this works:

1. Show great love to the happy people.

2. Show diligent action to the semi-happy people.

3. Show the door to the perpetually unhappy or harmful people.

You know who the happy people are—they are the ones being respectful of you, the staff and facilities. They cannot wait to see you, attend your events or rave about you and your services to friends or on Facebook®, Twitter® and LinkedIn®.

The semi-happy are doing similar things but maybe not as frequently or consistently. Their visits or purchases may have decreased because of a specific incident or misunderstanding. A courtesy email, phone call or timely lunchtime chat could bring clarity and rectify the situation, transferring them into the happy people category forever.

Then there are the perpetually unhappy or harmful. Before you label my solution as unreasonable or harsh, remember that similar measures take place every day in airports, restaurants and bars. Sometimes, you perform the greatest service by saying goodbye to the disgruntled, dastardly or dangerous. On a few occasions, I have had to do what I have described. I have encountered some ICs and ECs who seemed determined to stir up trouble and bring chaos to the work environment.

Being in key leadership positions, it was my responsibility to restore peace and order. Occasionally, I have recommended dismissal, offered contact information to competitors' establishments or summoned law enforcement. I firmly believe that when you show you are devoted to your customers' safety and enjoyment, they are more likely to show you their love and loyalty.

• **Connection—the "how we feel together" component.** "We" is the operative word. It is about relationships—it is *always* about relationships! This factor naturally flows from the "care" component, but it goes one step further by addressing your attachment to one another. Fostering shared respect and understanding with firm adherence to civility and manners contributes to creating positive, mutually beneficial connections.

Actively seeking customers' input and implementing their ideas—even if it is for a short test period—communicates to ICs and ECs that you are listening and treasure their expertise and involvement in your business.

• **Customization—the "how you're unique" component.** The wisdom found in the clichés, "Jack-of-all-trades, master of none" and "A mile wide, and an inch deep," speaks to the importance of customization. I was a public library director for more than five years and had several libraries offering similar services near mine. I lacked the budget, large staff and longevity the others had, but I was determined to set my library apart and make it outstanding and attractive. I accomplished this by regularly developing new services, securing nationally-known celebrities, and purchasing items the others would not. My library surged out of anonymity and mediocrity and became the happening place in the community—all through customization.

Focus on a core product or service that separates you from the crowd. Perhaps you will change the material composition of certain merchandise, or re-enter a "discarded" market and establish a new niche. Choose whatever makes you undeniably different, better, more desirable or encourages people to take notice, stay tuned and pursue you.

Chick-fil-A®, for example, is a successful franchise that serves mainly chicken products. There are no burgers, tacos or barbeque on their menu. They have chosen not to have a menu that's "a mile wide and an inch deep"; instead, they focus on serving quality chicken items. The result is excellent food and leadership in the quick-service industry. This organization also distinguishes itself by purposely closing one day a week—Sundays. That is customization!

Your Duty Is to Delight

Nothing gives more credence to your commitment to the $P^3+C^3=SCS!^{™}$ model than diligently applying all six elements. Listed below are some tangible ways you can demonstrate them. My categories and suggestions are not meant to be all-inclusive, but to give you a launching pad to develop your own creative, complementary ideas.

Ways to Delight Your Internal Customers

Would you like to reduce ICs' discouragement, exhaustion, apathy and turnover? You can by anticipating and meeting their needs. Here are some ideas that will make a difference:

• **Fundamentals.** Honesty, accountability, malleability, consistency and patience are some of the key principles for a trust-filled environment where emotional and professional security grow. Do you, your leadership and your business encourage and model these attributes? If not, examine, explore and correct the deficiencies.

• **Financial.** Look for—or establish—ways to get more cash in ICs' hands. Examples include promotions, incentive pay, longevity bonuses, merit pay, cost-of-living adjustments, step raises, employee recognition rewards or cost-savings awards. Remember, you fund what you value.

- **Free time.** Everybody likes time off. Review your policies and procedures for personal, vacation and sick-time allocations. When appropriate, allow overtime and comp-time. Consider adding extra holidays like Good Friday, Columbus Day, Martin Luther King, Jr. Day or others to your annual calendar. This way, ICs have more flexibility, and you are contributing to a healthy work-life balance—an attractive feature to prospective ICs.

- **Feel-goods.** Speak or write frequent and sincere thank you notes. Celebrate birthdays with paper or electronic cards, cakes or balloons. When a sickness or death occurs, send flowers and condolences. These small things tell ICs you think of them as individuals with lives outside the office.

Consider personally supplying the funds for these feel-goods if need be. I have made this a practice in every organization I have worked in. I have seen the delight caused by my giving birthday treats, Christmas presents or "just because" mementos to teammates. I guarantee that your personal investment on behalf of your ICs will reap you and your business long-term dividends.

- **Fun.** Introduce staff fun days, eat-and-meets, Friday night fun, company picnics or bowling parties. Get creative. I know a major corporation that shuts down for its annual picnic. Every employee gets to enjoy food, fun and fellowship while on the company's time. This is a good way to increase care and connection components.

Incorporating fun into the workplace does not have to be expensive or elaborate. The most modest activities can break routine monotony, make fond memories and build camaraderie. I have hosted many staff functions in my home, resulting in greater understanding and deeper, long-lasting relationships.

Ways to Delight Your External Customers

Want to get more people "through the door" and "dollars in the drawer?" Try these strategies with ECs:

- **Fundamentals.** The same honesty, accountability, malleability, consistency and patience apply here. Your truth-in-advertising, openness to change and reliability go a long way; expectations are high, ensuring you have a solid, value-filled operational platform.

- **Free stuff.** Who doesn't like getting something free? BOGOs—buy one, get one—dollars off, percentages off, whatever you're giving away, make sure it will be perceived as worthwhile to the customer. Nobody wants or needs second-rate items or offers. Giving away junk reflects poorly on you and your business.

  On my website, www.fearlessleading.com, I have a page where visitors register for a weekly drawing for a free personal or professional growth item. I make sure we give away only high-quality materials because I want winners to have something they deem necessary and valuable.

- **Follow-up.** What do you do when confronted with concerns or complaints? I advise adopting an "admit, apologize and be accountable" attitude over one that is "deny, defer and don't respond."

  How do you respond when complimented, and what tools do you use to keep those positive conversations going? Some effective demonstrations are emails, personally-signed letters, telephone calls, coupons, gift certificates and the like. Simple rewards and incentives tell them that you are in tune and in touch.

- **Feel-goods.** Though it can be more of a challenge to execute, ECs appreciate receiving personalized emails, text messages, cards and letters for a birthday, anniversary or notable event. Take advantage of auto-generating devices and electronic calendars to help with this. Of course, smiling, using their preferred names and remembering important details all make people feel cherished and strengthen your bond with them.

- **Fun.** Contests, promotions, carnivals and festivals are a few examples of how to incorporate fanfare into your business. Some establishments' employees break into song or dance if a secret word is spoken or if clients are celebrating a special event. It is fun to have fun.

Go for It!

You know that having an incredible business involves work and dedication, and delivering outstanding customer service does, too. Competition is fierce, and every organization is looking for ways to capture the hearts, minds or dollars of those around you. To be the one who successfully accomplishes this, you need a plan of action. You have received one today.

You now have a great model to enable you to get maximum impact from your customer service motto and effectively turn that maxim into advantageous action. Therefore, before the next business day ends, memorize the formula: $P^3 + C^3 = SCS!^{™}$.

Review the six components:

- Presentation

- Personality

- Programming

- Care

- Connection

- Customization

Evaluate your current customer service activities and practices. Gather and solicit input from others. Get brutally honest with yourself to see if what you are doing aligns with the components above. Then administer massive doses of each component and get ready for increased sales, positive PR, happier staff with less conflict and more pride of ownership, improved ability to attract and retain superior talent, gains in market share, and much, much more—essentially providing sensational customer service inside and out.

VICTORIA ASHFORD
Fearless Leadership

*Getting you mentally conditioned
and properly positioned!*

(205) 620-1006
victoria@fearlessleading.com
www.fearlessleading.com

A sought-after speaker, trainer and coach, Victoria provides high-energy, entertaining presentations, sessions and workshops after which all participants leave equipped, encouraged and empowered. Her practical and timely motivational programs on leadership development, customer service and courage cultivation have reached and benefited a vast and assorted audience. She has spoken to professionals in small business, human resources, banking, public library, nonprofit, higher education and governmental sectors. She masterfully weaves amusing anecdotes and insights together for a memorable event.

A take-charge, multi-faceted woman, Victoria gleans and mines great lessons from her experiences as an educator, library director, GED examiner and Air Force officer. In her spare time, she is a successful real estate investor and winter sports enthusiast.

Victoria founded and leads Excelcis Training & Consulting, Inc. She has a bachelor of arts degree from the University of Arizona and a master of arts degree from the University of Alabama at Birmingham. Victoria has been sharing her innovative methods and messages, improving the lives and performance of individuals, fostering effective team development and increasing their productivity or sales since 1988.

Beyond the Art of Listening
Paralanguage Skills for Profit and Persuasion
By Suzanne Zazulak Pedro, CPC

"Communication is something so simple and difficult
that we can never put it in simple words."
—T.S. Matthews, American journalist,
past editor of *Time* magazine

*L*anguage is the song to which the universe dances, and is a key communications vehicle. It is a way of expressing ideas, of shared understanding. Hence, the appearance of a language is the beginning or birth of a shared understanding that represents a community, whether a family, business organization or culture.

Albert Mehrabian, a pioneer in nonverbal communication research, found that only 7 percent of a message's effects are conveyed in words; listeners receive the other 93 percent through nonverbal meaning. Furthermore, 91 percent of workplace confusion is due to poor communication.

There is correlation between effective communication, productivity and a company's bottom line. To effectively communicate, you need to go beyond words and use paralanguage listening, which covers the verbal (linguistics) as well as the nonverbal clues (elements) to modify meaning and convey emotion. Speaking the right words has to be in context with all of the other elements of communication, otherwise confusion and dissonance result. To avoid miscommunication in business and life, the following strategies and information can help you hone your skills in paralanguage listening—a world beyond the text of words that uses all of your senses when communicating.

Bees Do It

Every species' genetic composition allows them to effectively communicate with other members of their species—and even with their enemies. For example, communication and survival for honeybees depends upon their unique ability to decipher different ways to communicate. In 330 B.C., Athenian philosopher Aristotle first noticed honeybee workers perform a sophisticated series of movements affectionately known as the "waggle" dance. When the scout bees find sources of food like pollen and nectar, chemo-receptors on their bodies communicate to other bees by depositing scent and by the scout bees dancing on the honeycomb. Bees can discern the distance from their hive to the source of food and communicate that information by the vigorous shaking of their abdomens and by producing a buzzing sound with the beat of their wings. The distance and speed of this movement communicates the distance of the foraging site to others by the use of acoustics, vibration and haptics—the science of touch.

It is not only animals that effectively communicate. Plants and bacteria do, too. When under attack from animals, plants release chemicals that appear to cause neighboring plants to alter the composition of their leaves so they become more toxic. Chemical conversations between bacteria play a central role in some human diseases; whether we want to communicate with them or not, the diseases, unfortunately, communicate with us.

If bees, plants and even bacteria do it, why do we, with our higher cognitive abilities, have a difficult time communicating with each other? Unlike other species, our communication is a learned skill, and we need to use all of our faculties to avoid miscommunication.

Listening Versus Hearing—A Learned Human Skill

Listening is one of the most important skills you can possess. It is vitally important for any type of leadership. However, there is little emphasis or instruction in our school system. Experience tells us that just because you hear something does not mean you were listening.

While hearing is basically an involuntary physical act, listening is the interactive, emotional and intellectual act of hearing not only what is said, but it also includes responding to both the verbal and nonverbal message. If you dare to ask why you should be a better listener, the answer is that it promotes credibility, persuasion and the leadership skills necessary to be successful in business and life.

The Costs of Miscommunication

As a business leader or head of an organization, it is important to realize that miscommunication is costly to you as a person in leadership, and to an organization financially, and it is a backlash for the consumer with the rising costs of commodities. According to a September 2009 article in PeopleMetrics®, the Joint Commission, an organization that serves the health care industry, reported that miscommunication "harms an estimated 1.5 million people in the United States each year, and results in upwards of $3.5 billion in extra medical costs" in the health care industry alone.

In June 2009, the Global Business and Economic Round Table on Addiction and Mental Health reported that lack of two-way communication is the number two cause of stress in the American workplace. This is reason enough to learn to be a better listener and effectively communicate with others.

Active listening occurs when you make a conscious effort to not just "hear" the words being spoken, or what you want to hear, but also listen for the intent and the nonverbal communication of the speaker.

When you use paralanguage listening, you use your skills of empathy and emotion to be nonjudgmental. For example, listening is a necessary element in the sales industry. If you do not listen, you can't close the sale because you won't know what the customer wants. You can make a costly mistake by not properly listening to your customer's order. Since people tend to buy for emotional reasons, you want to take into consideration the customer's body language.

Would you like to know from reading "paralanguage" listening how to persuade an individual to take the winning sales step and close the deal? If so, follow an iconic symbol, the 400-year-old Japanese image for a 2,500-year-old ancient Chinese code for conduct—Three Monkeys: See No Evil, Hear No Evil and Speak No Evil.

The visual image of the three monkeys espouses the proverb, "The wise man in communicating is prudent in what he looks for, what he listens to and what he speaks." For effective communication in your next sales discussion, look for those important nonverbal clues, listen beyond the words being said and watch your semantics when speaking.

See No Evil

Research shows that reading facial expressions is a neglected activity in communication. Dr. Paul Ekman, renowned psychologist and co-author of *Emotion in the Human Face,* published in 1971 by Pergamon Press, determined that everyone in the world shares and recognizes seven basic facial emotions: happiness, sadness, fear, surprise, anger, contempt and disgust. Since each emotion has a unique discernable facial signal, this is the only system that communicates these specific emotions.

This is important at work; it is the part of active listening where you assess the speaker's more overt facial expressions and become more intuitive about the underlying subconscious emotions. This is essential in effective leadership communication. Here are a few tips for face reading.

Eye Contact

- An attentive listener will hold eye contact approximately seventy percent of the time, but often the time spent "listening" is the amount of time required to gather our own thoughts. It is more beneficial to use your time focusing on the speaker rather than on your next thought.

- Create an imaginary triangle with the eyes at the base and the apex at mid-forehead for the "look of business"—business gaze. When you keep your gaze in that area, you nonverbally transmit a no-nonsense, businesslike approach.

- When people think, different parts of their brain are accessed depending upon the type of information sought. For instance, when right-handers are creating an image—a "gorilla" in the room—their eyes generally look up and to the right. However, if they are recalling something they've heard like an old melody, they look to the left and tilt their head as though listening. If they are remembering either a physical or emotional sensation, they look down and to the right. People talking silently to themselves also look down but to the left. This is an excellent test of rapport with your client or employee. For instance, if you tell your customer to imagine himself behind the wheel, notice the direction of his eyes.

Do you see them go down and to the right, trying to remember a feeling or up and right trying to picture himself in the car. If not, you may need to change your sales tactics.

Speak No Evil

A master communicator looks for different clues provided by paralanguage listening. No matter what you say, it is always subject to interpretation and the perspective of the listener. Do you remember the game of "Gossip" in your early school days? In this game, you told one person a juicy piece of gossip that each person then communicated to another. By the time the information went around the circle or the office grapevine, the content and context was different from the initial statement. This is also known as the "Dual Reality Principle," when two people hear the same thing, but each comes to different conclusions. How many times has this happened to you in your office?

A boss's innocuous statement to his secretary can be interpreted as offensive without any clear reason. This usually happens by allowing emotional and mental filters to affect your listening. For example, answering a call after an intense argument will hamper your ability to listen since your mind will still be on the argument. That is your reality, while the caller may gather that you are uninterested or rude. To enhance your skills as a listener, be aware of the types of filters and learn how to detach yourself from them.

Persuade with Language Patterns

Here are some tips to help you use language as a tool for persuasion, courtesy of Dr. Milton Erickson, a psychologist and the father of Ericksonian hypnosis. This is a collection of language patterns that are examples of how you can make suggestions without giving a commanding order, and in a way that meets your needs.

• Use past, present and future verb tenses to change people's minds by taking them on a time-travel adventure. By using this method, one could take a problem that is in the present tense and speak of it in the past perfect tense as if it were over and done. For example, *I am procrastinating* (present issue), *I was procrastinating* (past issue), *I had procrastinated* (past perfect). This takes a present problem and makes it feel different using the past perfect. Speaking of a present problem and referring to it in the past tense helps the listener think that it is no longer a problem.

• "Sleight-of-Mouth" was coined by Robert Dilts, the co-founder of NeuroLinguistic Programming (NLP), who never lost an argument with this tactic. The technique uses succinct comments and questions designed to attack the very core of a belief and remove it, or at the very least, question it. This also can be used to reinforce existing beliefs. Carefully listen for an individual's belief. Once you have identified the belief to be changed or loosened, proceed to use a volley of four or five sleight-of-mouth patterns to produce an entirely new perspective. For example:

Belief: Customer: "I will have to talk to my boss to make the decision."

Sleight-of-Mouth: Salesperson: "Could it be that you have never considered the amount of decision-making ability that your boss has already bestowed upon you?"

This begins to loosen the person's belief that they cannot make the decision without consulting with their boss.

Hear No Evil

Language is a representational system for our experiences and emotions, past, present and future. We all learn and process information with three different types of learning modalities. These learning styles, or sensory modalities, are visual, auditory and kinesthetic. If someone says, "I cannot wrap my head around this problem," you know that their learning process is kinesthetic. You can now structure your replies with the same tone, words and thoughts to establish rapport by mirroring his words and emotions. If they use words that relate to hearing, such as "Let's talk about this" or "I hear you," they are auditory. If they use visual words, like "Show me" or "Let's see where this goes," they are visual.

Here are some non-verbal tips to improve your listening skills:

• Listen for the intent of the speaker in nonverbal clues. For example, "Isn't that nice" can be said with a tone of sarcasm or with sincerity. Is the verbal message consistent with the nonverbal message? If not, clarify the speaker's meaning.

• Pay attention to the pitch, rate and volume of the speaker. This will give you a view into their emotional state. For example, if the speaker is talking more rapidly, higher and louder than usual, it is safe to assume that he or she is nervous which gives you insight into their emotional state. You can now change your behavior to ease the situation.

• Be aware of your own vocal cues when responding. Remember, it is not what you say that people hear, it is how they hear you say it—the tone, emphasis and pitch. However, if your nonverbal actions oppose your spoken words, the message sent can be misinterpreted. Make sure your language and nonverbal clues align.

From Soup to Nuts

There are companies today that use psychological communication concepts to reach their target market audience. It is called Neuro-Marketing®. For example, Campbell's® knew that their soup elicited emotional feelings. How many of you were given a warm, steaming bowl of chicken noodle soup when you were sick or cold? The company specifically uses biometrics that measure the customer's pupil dilation—positive sign—when eating their soup. The biometric monitoring showed this warmth faded in the supermarket soup aisle when the consumer was confronted with a wall of nearly identical red and white cans. Consequently, their advertising executives were able to unlock their customers' brains and revamp their advertising campaign to increase sales.

In business and leadership, you need to become a master communicator and a "supersuader"—a super persuader. Paralanguage listening is an important factor in the art of conversation and persuasion. It is an effective business tool to help you become aware of what was previously an unnoticed process. Instead of just having a positive or negative feeling about someone, such as an employee or customer, noticing body signals will give you insight so you can decide whether your conclusions are valid.

Paralanguage listening is also your guide to creating dynamism and projecting a powerful image. Become an excellent listener and communicator of both verbal and nonverbal language—an expert at paralanguage listening—and people will perceive you to have a highly-valued status, to be competent and effective, and to be a high-intensity persona. These are all the qualities necessary to be powerfully persuasive and influential. Your good reputation will then precede you.

SUZANNE ZAZULAK PEDRO, CPC
The Protocol Praxis, LLC

(985) 974-0947
suzanne@theprotocolpraxis.com
www.theprotocolpraxis.com

Suzanne Zazulak Pedro, CPC, co-author of *Executive Etiquette Power* and a Behavior Shaping Specialist, has crafted her academic qualifications and her certifications in professional executive coaching and corporate etiquette into a cutting-edge approach called Neuro-Etiquette™. Neuro-Etiquette is powered by psychological applications and protocol for success-based behavior in business and personal finesse.

As founder of The Protocol Praxis, LLC, Suzanne is a Certified Hypnotherapist and is completing her Master Certification in Neuro Linguistic Programming. She has crafted her talent in physiognomy and in micro-expressions to give her clients a wide range of tools for discovering positive behavior and delivering panache into their lifestyles.

In addition to serving as Chief Officer of Protocol and monthly Etiquette columnist for her city, she has formed a non-profit organization, BeePoised, and acts as counselor and advocate for women and children. Suzanne's professional memberships include The International Society of Protocol & Etiquette Professionals, *Cambridge's Who's Who Among Entrepreneurs* and The National Writers Union. She holds a bachelor of arts degree in psychology from Loyola University, and is engaged in completing her masters in contemporary diplomacy.

Become a Leader Who Grows People
By Suzie Read

Self-esteem is the lifeblood of performance at work. When your employees or team members feel good about themselves and their environment, they do more and are more engaged in their work. Sometimes managers and business owners see direct reports as people below them in the hierarchy, and therefore they do not recognize the importance of self-esteem to their workers. Good managers and business owners, on the other hand, show trust, openness and respect toward employees and team members and lavish authentic praise and freedom of choice on them. In this kind of environment, people succeed and their self-esteem increases. This means that to become a leader who grows people, you must become others-centered, rather than self-centered.

Some people walk through life with themselves as the center of their circle. They are the stars of their own show. They care about others and want to be others-centered but are driven more by what makes *them* happy.

Many things drive behavior to be self-centered or others-centered. Your values drive you to behave a certain way. Most of the time, this is positive. If you want money, you work hard. If you have a goal, you are willing to learn and try new things to reach that goal. If you love your family, you make them a priority. However, when actions are based on fear or a negative way of thinking or being, negative emotions—insecurities, fears, doubts, negative beliefs—override positive emotions, and people get stuck in self-centeredness.

The key to being a leader and growing people is to recognize when this happens and to step outside of the center of the circle and move away from self-centeredness. When you do this, your business can begin to flourish, and your dream becomes bigger than you are. This is the sweet spot—you do more and are more because you care more.

> *"If your actions inspire others to dream more, learn more, do more and become more, you are a leader."*
> —John Quincy Adams, sixth President of the United States

There are four parts to becoming a leader who grows people.

Part One: Be Willing to Move out of the Center of Your Circle

You have to be willing to move out of the center of your circle. When you are in the center of the circle, your dream will never be realized, nor will it ever be big enough.

Awareness of where you are in your circle is the first thing to recognize. Once you have awareness, you can then take responsibility for your choices and your actions. Awareness happens through focused attention, concentration and clarity.

How do you know when you are in the center, and it is not healthy? You will find yourself having critical, negative conversations with and about people. You may say something like, "My team is lazy. I can't motivate them to do anything," or, "I know I need to reprimand her for her actions, but I don't want to look like the bitchy boss."

If you want to change your results, you need to change your conversations. When you step outside of the center and put others in the center, the conversations change. You might instead say, "I love developing relationships with my team to the extent that they feel ownership for the business and become self-motivated," or, "It's my job as her boss to be honest with her about her actions so she can learn and grow from this experience." The conversations are less about benefiting oneself and more about benefiting the other person.

When you find yourself saying something that is self-centered, turn the switch and restate it to be others-centered. This will take time to become a habit, but you can make a huge difference in how you relate to your team with this simple change.

Part Two: Be Willing to Understand Them

As leaders in the workplace, a key element to leadership is to fully understand the person in front of you. Not many people show up for work planning to be a bad employee or planning to have a bad attitude. They may show up this way because of what is going on in their lives.

People sometimes ask, "What's wrong with that person? Why can't they figure it out?" Well, maybe that person has been beaten up by life. Somewhere along the way, someone told him or her, "You can't do it," "You don't know enough," or, "You are not enough." On the other hand, maybe the individual has just had a lot of pain in his or her life. In addition, our lives are unfortunately not like pizzas where we cut them up into different slices—each slice separate from another. When something happens in one area, it will absolutely carry over into other areas.

One way to better understand your employees and team is to recognize that every person has dreams and hopes. Asking questions helps you gather information, develop rapport with people and clarify the real issues. A good question can make a person think. It honors the other person's intelligence and empowers them, slows down automatic thinking and responses and helps keep them focused.

When asking questions, use open-ended questions that need more than a yes or no answer. Here are some different types of questions you may want to ask to learn more about the other person.

Situational Questions

• What obstacles kept you from meeting your goal last month?

• What considerations do you have in setting your goal for this week? With those considerations in mind, what help will you need to accomplish your goal?

Inquiry Questions

• How much money do you want to make this month?

• How important is it for you to hit your goals?

• How will you feel if you do not hit your goal?

Action Questions

• What are some things you can do to overcome these obstacles?

• When will you do that?

• How can I support you?

Thought-Provoking Questions

• I have always wondered why some weeks it is easier to do the actions I know will help me to hit my goal. What are your thoughts about achieving consistency in hitting your goal? I know when I'm not certain I can do the job, I tend to procrastinate. What makes you procrastinate?

• What do you think holds you back from getting into action?

Feeling Questions

• How do you feel when you don't hit your goal?

• How do you think your attitude affects your ability to hit your goal?

• What will it feel like when you get that promotion?

To connect with people and have them feel truly valued, use and repeat the key words and phrases they use. Listen to their language. It may not be comfortable for you, but they will hear you better. Very often, it is not a difference in language that separates us; it is the judgment we impose on the language. For more information on how to use and understand language, see the chapter *Beyond the Art of Listening* by Suzanne Zazulak Pedro on page 149.

The next part of understanding someone is probably the most difficult. You can ask all the questions you want, but understanding requires you to listen to the answers. There is a big difference between *hearing* what someone says and *listening* to what someone says. When you are listening, you:

• Think about what the person is saying, not your response.

• Stay focused on the speaker and avoid distractions.

• Stay on the subject and do not try to dominate the conversation.

• Use appropriate facial expressions and gestures to indicate interest.

• Ask questions to fully understand what they are saying.

Start conversations with, "I want to hear what you have to say" to set an intention to listen and ask questions that paraphrase the speaker's comments. Paraphrasing ensures that you understand the content the way the speaker intended, and it signals the speaker that you are actively listening. For example:

• Tell me more...

• How did you feel when...?

• If I understand you correctly...

• You are saying that...

• What was your reaction to...?

• What I hear you say is...

As a leader, you must think of people in terms of their potential, not their performance. See each person as someone who can be more if they choose. Give them the opportunity to learn from mistakes. This gives them the opportunity for positive change and growth.

When you look at people in terms of their performance, you may tend to put them in "performance boxes." When you put people into performance boxes, it is hard for them to escape—either in their eyes or in yours.

Part Three: Be Willing to Serve

The third aspect to being a leader who grows people is to be willing to serve. Serving others can be inconvenient. It requires you to be others-centered, which requires patience, time, compassion and empathy. That to which you give your time is what you value, and when you give your time to people, they feel like they matter.

Where can you serve people better and with greater focus? Is it in spending more time with them having meaningful conversations?

Sometimes, you can serve others by just caring about them and what they want more than what you want.

When I was 29 years old, I was fired from a job. As a top achiever all of my life, I was humiliated. Imagine, me—fired! One of the things my boss said to me was that he knew I did not like my job, that I was only in it because it was a safe place for me to be. My being in that job was not good for the company and it was not good for me. He was letting me go to give me the opportunity to find what I truly wanted.

At the time, I did not see his wisdom. Now, looking back, he gave me a gift. It was because of that experience that I found direct sales and experienced extreme self-growth, financial success and lots of fun. That boss truly served me by letting me go.

To serve others first, be willing. Second, know what matters to them by taking the time to know them. Then care enough about them to help them get what they want.

"What we do for ourselves dies with us.
What we do for others and the world remains and is immortal."
—Albert Pine, American author

Part Four: Be Honest

The fourth, and probably most important, aspect of being a leader who grows people is honesty. For the most part, in the business world, you have surface relationships based on what people do versus who they are or who they are going to become. To be a great leader who grows people, honest conversations are necessary. If what you say and what you do are not congruent, your employees and team members will not feel safe when having crucial conversations with you. In fact, they will not respect what you have to say.

To have an honest conversation, you first need to look at who you are. Integrity can be defined as showing behavior that instills trust. Do your life and your actions back up what you are saying? If so, great. People will feel safe when you have crucial conversations with them.

Are you real with them? Do you admit your faults and struggles and are you willing to be a bit vulnerable with them? Share with them where you struggled and learned a lesson. Your employees and team will trust you more if they know you have been in their shoes and learned from that experience.

Setting expectations is another opportunity you have to demonstrate honesty with people. Setting expectations is not just telling people what to do. While everyone needs to know what actions they need to take and what responsibilities they have on the job, we set expectations for people when we know what they want or what their goals are. For example, ask people where they see themselves in a year or two or what their goals are. Taking the time to ask, setting expectations for their advancement and assisting them in planning to achieve what they want is crucial to their success. During the "setting the expectations" part, there are two key words to know: awareness and responsibility.

When people have awareness, they know how to notice their own stuff—how to feel what is happening in their mind and in their body so they can improve themselves without someone else telling them to. Awareness builds self-reliance, self-belief, self-confidence and self-responsibility.

Responsibility is crucial for high performance. When you truly accept, choose or take responsibility for your thoughts and your actions, your commitment to them rises and so does your performance. To feel truly responsible, you can then choose your actions and your reactions. The same is true for your employees and team members.

Awareness and responsibility go hand-in-hand. Once you have awareness of why you do what you do, you can then take responsibility and choose to change your actions, if need be.

> *"Honesty is the cornerstone of all success, without which confidence and ability to perform shall cease to exist."*
> —Mary Kay Ash, American entrepreneur
> and founder of Mary Kay® Inc.

People matter. They are worth the time you invest in them. If you want a healthy work environment, change your environment. To change your environment, change your conversations. Conversations with people are opportunities. When you give someone an opportunity for a conversation, you give them the possibility of growth and change. For more information on how to have meaningful conversations with all kinds of people, see the chapter *Taking Relationships to Referrals to Profit* by Mike Coy on page 191.

Start now to ask open-ended questions that uncover more information and encourage people to communicate honestly and candidly. Hone your listening skills and develop people. Become the leader you know you can be and lead your business to success.

SUZIE READ
Leadership Development Specialist

(360) 509-9470
suzie@suzieread.com
www.suzieread.com

Suzie Read began her direct sales career 14 years ago because she wanted to be there when her children got on and off the school bus, *and* she needed to earn an income. Beginning as a sales consultant, she learned quickly that direct sales offered an incredible avenue for changing lifestyles and lives. She is passionate about teaching women and men to laugh at themselves, love themselves and stretch themselves to be more, do more and give more of themselves to others.

Suzie has the ability to build and lead teams to high levels of performance. She specializes in fun, dynamic trainings that teach others to book full calendars, sell more products, sponsor more people and develop more leaders. Suzie also offers coaching to individuals and groups.

As a highly regarded speaker, coach and motivator who connects with people, Suzie has held the positions of national recruiter, communications director, director of field training and, most recently, regional sales director for Willow House, a direct sales company. She is a Certified Dream Coach™, Dream Coach Group Leader™ and a member of Toastmaster's International®. Suzie lives near Seattle, Washington.

Developing Strategic Alliances
By Kathy Carrico

"Hitch your wagon to a star."
—Ralph Waldo Emerson,
American philosopher, essayist and poet

What I have found in my fifteen years with a government agency whose tagline is "business services network," is what defines the entrepreneur is the insatiable drive for knowledge, innovation and resources. People are the most strategic resource and when individuals align with one another, they create power.

Strategically working on your business makes you successful *in* your business. Whether you are running a large corporation or a micro-business, developing alliances needs to be a critical piece of your strategic plan. Every relationship and strategic alliance provides mutual benefits that can significantly affect your business growth. They help you increase the number of good players involved in making your business successful. Strategic alliances require you to identify people and businesses that want to work with you to achieve a common goal.

We all know there is power in numbers, and this certainly holds true in business. The resources you access can allow you to grow faster and smarter. In start-up and expansion stages, people who do not seek the advice and assistance of experts will typically take longer and circuitous steps to success because they try to do it alone. The same holds true in your operations.

A simple, key strategy is to form an advisory board that can be as basic as a small group of your most trusted business contacts who want to help you. One way to manage this would be to hold a quarterly two-hour meeting with an itemized agenda and a clear definition of what you hope to accomplish. Give your board some action steps to report on prior to your meeting. Be the facilitator and engage your board on strategic initiatives. As long as you do not ask for too much time, and they feel their time is valued, they will come back. This group will be instrumental in helping you move forward in identifying strategic alliances.

Creating Your Value

Many experts state that the prime consideration in forming strategic alliances must be, "What's in it for me?" I advise my clients to first consider, "What's in it for *them*?"

In order to answer this critically important question, you need to establish your personal "reputation of value" through strong standards of excellence in the areas of credibility, integrity and relevant knowledge. You cannot form any meaningful relationship, partner-ship, venture or alliance until you align with yourself and your value. Be confident in the value you portray and believe that what you bring to the table is exceptional in every way. You will then be in a position to deliberately and strategically create win-win alliances.

Your business consistently provides a quality product or service. That's a given. Now, answer these questions.

• What else makes you better than your competitors?

• What can make you the best?

• How do you go about creating real and perceived value?

• How do you sustain that value?

Large corporations intentionally and strategically establish a reputation of value all the time, and it affects why people become loyal customers. According to an article by Klaus Kneale, posted October 22, 2009, on forbes.com, "Corporate giving programs are a big deal these days…. During tough times, reputation is everything. A survey by Boston College's Center for Corporate Citizenship and the Hitachi Foundation found that seventy percent of senior executives considered reputation the number-one driver behind their companies' corporate citizenship efforts."

Share your values. It helps to identify and align with nonprofits who share similar values. A woman in my community is a fabulous professional speaker, coach and animal lover. She started a nonprofit association that helps raise money to feed sheltered animals. She works directly with the humane society and when she provides a keynote or any other type of presentation, she tells her audience about her charitable cause. By doing this, she helps animals, gains a compassionate audience and allows others to experience a personal side of her that matters to society.

Another friend is a newspaper publisher who works tirelessly to promote our annual Juvenile Diabetes Research Foundation golf tournament. He has a child with Type I diabetes and is passionate about increasing public awareness. When my own son was diagnosed with the same disease in 2008, this friend was the first person I contacted for support and guidance.

Aligning yourself with good causes is powerful, and it can take many forms.

• **Use your hobby to find volunteer work.** For example, if you have expertise in gardening, you can contact your local community college and offer to lead a workshop on how to grow awesome vegetables in the backyard.

- **You can use your business knowledge.** For example, if you are a makeup artist, you can volunteer your talents at the local high school the afternoon of the senior prom and do makeovers for young women.

- **It does not take expertise to help.** Senior centers are full of lonely people who would love someone to spend some time with them. You could take a few photos and write a short article about how special your new senior friend is.

- **Getting involved with a chamber of commerce** and joining the welcoming committee at business events is a win-win. You will meet potential clients and help the chamber at the same time.

- **If you have a company with employees,** take a half-day off annually and volunteer your company's time and talent for a good cause. Not only do you get out into the community, your employees can gain some solid teamwork skills themselves. Entrepreneurs have very little time to spare, but it is important to get involved if only for a few hours each year.

Spread the news. What happens once you donate your talent? You have just increased your value, and others should know about it. Do you have a blog on your website, or even better, do your friends write blogs? The good news about you is best received from outside sources. Take plenty of photos, write a press release, get some testimonials or put a video clip on your website. Create a reputation of giving and do not be shy as the world learns about you. You may inadvertently influence others to follow, and this may be a determining factor in who chooses to accept you as their strategic ally!

> *"Let someone else acknowledge your virtues."*
> *(Waiho ma te tangata e mihi.)*
> —New Zealand Maori proverb

Adopt best practices. Three simple best practices that can make or break your value.

1. Be on time.

2. Come prepared.

3. Return phone calls and emails.

These sound simple, but think of your circle of friends and business associates. How many of them violate one or more of these best practices? Does it affect how you feel, and whether you hesitate in doing repeat business with them?

Alliances are short-lived by those who do not take these three steps seriously. Respect for these practices reflects your overall integrity.

Set a standard of excellence. How much time do you take, and how do you rate your performance in the things you do and the services you provide? Looking back on standard report cards or employee evaluations, you will notice that they range from poor to satisfactory, to good and excellent. To anyone who prides himself or herself on being a perfectionist, think again. Have you ever seen a measurement of perfection? I seriously doubt it! Perfection is unattainable, and those who seek this level ultimately waste precious time. By adopting standards of excellence, you will absolutely know when to move on and get the most out of your time.

Grow your knowledge base. Your knowledge base is relevant and proportionate to your value. How do you keep up with your industry, your profession and technology? What tools are you using to gain efficiency in learning? There is tremendous benefit in joining industry and professional associations. Identify them and become a member. Subscribe to traditional or online newsletters.

Now, more than ever, you have the opportunity to meet people nationally and globally through new media platforms. Find a few key blogs and read them religiously. Provide comments and join the conversations. Network with fellow members and meet them at conferences or conventions. Submit an article and make sure it is excellent. The silver lining behind all of this is that you force yourself to conduct research. In the process of reading and writing, you gain immediate and valuable knowledge.

How can you create value? Review the information in this section and set a goal for creating value.

Identifying Your Strategic Alliances

When you are a leading expert in your industry and your profession, you provide value to everything you touch. Now is the time to identify and recognize your ideal strategic allies. Remember, you do not form alliances with a company, business, corporation, subsidiary, agency, institution, association, affiliation or group. You connect with individuals, and that is where the real power lies.

Check out your database of business acquaintances and think about who shares a similar target market with you. Focus on the main objective of sharing a common goal and start the conversation. Begin forming new alliances with people you already know and trust.

Continue to build your database from word-of-mouth referrals and people about whom you read in news articles that blend with your values and goals. Extend an invitation to meet in person at a time and place convenient for your potential new ally. Come prepared to sell your value, and present your plan that creates a win-win venture.

I recall a man leaving a voice message that briefly introduced himself as the new department director of a company with which I was familiar. His voice was confident, his message was short and his purpose was clear. He referenced a recent newspaper article about a program I ran and complimented my success. He asked me for thirty minutes of my time to discuss our similar market and explore some options that would provide mutual benefit. I looked him up on his company's website and was thrilled to move forward. Since that meeting, we entered into a number of successful projects and continue to embrace the value of working together.

Several years ago, I was invited to participate in a presentation to a state agency that was funding business development education. The competition was fierce, but I knew our products and services were top shelf. In addition to providing a short PowerPoint overview, I donated a full set of materials to the agency and offered a complimentary seat in our 13-week course. We continue to receive funding from this agency.

Align to expand your network. You are ready to identify potential alliances for your business. If you are a sole proprietor or micro-business, you may think about aligning with others of the same size. Instead, think about who is bigger, smarter and more profitable than you. For example, if you have a service business and offer consulting, coaching, training, counseling and so on, consider aligning with a chamber of commerce, an economic development affiliation, a large business or a state or federal agency.

Check out their website and see what they are *not* offering that would provide a member or community benefit. After you have done your research, attend their events and see where your expertise could provide value. Network with people you meet at these events. Identify the decision makers and the individuals who are behind the scenes. Get to know them and ask questions about who they are, what their roles involve and let them get to know you. Take the time to build personal relationships.

Just last year, I was in a meeting with some people from our state's Department of Veterans Affairs. We were discussing the importance of self-employment for returning veterans, and I mentioned our training program that teaches applied entrepreneurial practices while writing a business plan. That meeting resulted in another meeting with decision makers who were elated to make this course available to their clients. Through a memorandum of understanding, we became an official vendor of entrepreneurial education for their clients across the entire state.

Consider the network of followers associated with your potential alliances. A successful alignment can introduce and expose you to their networks.

Incorporate written contracts as needed. Once you establish a strategic alliance, you and your new ally can discuss if a contract is applicable to your venture. A contract can be important when money is exchanged, revenue is split or deadlines drive a deal. It should protect both parties and provide overall clarity of each party's responsibility. Examples would be a memorandum of understanding, a sub-agreement, a compensation plan, employment contract, intellectual property rights agreement, and so on.

Be entrepreneurial. In considering strategic alliances, creativity is key. Let's say you own a bakery, and you depend on walk-in traffic to sell your products. You may want to find someone who runs an event business that provides services for corporate functions, birthday parties, special events and more. Propose an alliance to provide the most unique or popular item you sell. Design your services to save them time by delivering to their events and price your product where you make a volume profit. For example, a colleague of mine was presenting a business seminar several months ago. A cabinetmaker in the audience was concerned that the economy had drastically affected the demand for his products and services. It was suggested that he form an alliance with a local pet store that sells puppies. Since puppies chew furniture, he could offer his furniture repair services at a discount to people who purchased puppies from the shop.

There are countless alignments to be made: a dry cleaner and tailor; a children's author and a public school system; a chamber of commerce and a local university; a city planning commission and a database management specialist. The list is endless.

Whom could you align with, and what value can you bring to the table?

Being the Magnet of Incredible Alliances

"I have found no greater satisfaction than achieving success through honest dealing and strict adherence to the view that, for you to gain, those you deal with should gain as well."
—Alan Greenspan, American economist
and former Federal Reserve chair

Identifying your best alliance partners is a key part of your business strategy. When you provide a higher-than-expected level of excellence and value, you become a valuable strategic ally to others. They will want to align with you.

It takes time, planning, consistency and follow-up. Track your success in a portfolio and grow it with each alliance you develop. This becomes a tool that showcases your value.

Love what you do, value the people around you and strive to make a positive difference. Attract those who do the same, and life becomes better, and your business becomes more incredible.

KATHY CARRICO
State Training Director,
NV Small Business Development Center

(775) 784-6879
kathycarrico@kathycarrico.com
www.kathycarrico.com

When Kathy Carrico received the opportunity to help small business owners through educational outreach, she quickly jumped out of operations and into what has become a fifteen-year training position with the Nevada Small Business Development Center at the University of Nevada, Reno.

In 1999, Kathy submitted a $50,000 proposal to fund entrepreneurship. Eleven years later and after almost $1 million in funding, Kathy has helped hundreds of small business owners get on board with the NxLeveL for Entrepreneurs® training throughout Nevada.

Kathy became well connected with the Northern Nevada Chamber of Commerce in 2004 by chairing several committees and providing expertise at chamber events. She was voted Chamber Member of the Year in 2005 and became an active board member in 2006. Kathy will serve as president of the chamber in 2011.

Kathy aligned her talents with the local Boys & Girls Club and in 2009 founded Campus Kids, a highly successful summer youth program, which has helped hundreds of kids experience a four-day university visit while learning leadership, entrepreneurship and the value of education. Kathy is a "business butterfly" in countless pursuits that have aligned her agency and herself with highly valuable and profitable strategic alliances.

How to Be Recognized as an Expert and Attract Clients with Ease

By Caterina Rando, MA, MCC

*I*n today's marketplace, any potential client can go online, type in two or three keywords, search Google® and immediately find whatever he or she is looking for, quickly reviewing a lifetime supply of vendors anxious to fill the person's request. Still, a potential client usually does not know who the best match is just by reviewing websites. That is good for savvy businesses that use value-added marketing. Value-added marketing allows your firm to differentiate itself in the marketplace and create a sense of certainty with your potential clients, allowing them to be sure that you and your company are the right solution.

Defining Value-Added Marketing

Value-added marketing is providing value to potential clients *before* you ask them to hire you. That's right! I am suggesting you give away a bit of your valuable expertise before a client has hired you. Why? Because when you freely give something of value, potential clients view you and your business differently. They recognize and appreciate your expertise and generosity. They know before they even meet you that you have something of value to offer them— something worth paying for. Value-added marketing gives you a competitive edge, showcases your expertise and establishes you as an expert. It also throws your marketing net far wider than your competitors who are only using traditional marketing methods like advertising, trade shows and direct mail. Value-added marketing truly allows you to attract clients with ease.

Get Started

When you embrace value-added marketing, you will be able to deliver your expertise around the clock in a variety of ways. Value-added marketing is easy to do once you get started, and, in some cases, it is even free.

Here are some of the different strategies you can employ to get your value-added marketing out there:

• Free teleclasses to share value and introduce yourself to potential clients

• Podcasts people can download and listen to anytime

• Blogging to share value on an ongoing basis

• Writing articles, posting them in article directories and on websites your potential clients visit

• Recording video and posting it on your website, video sites and social networking sites

• Delivering a live speech for free to a room full of your potential clients

• Free webinars

• Hosting or being a guest on a traditional or Internet radio show or Internet television show

While there are many ways to get your brilliant ideas out there, I encourage you to start with podcasts, teleclasses, live and in-person speeches and short videos.

Before we dive into how to get started with a few of these value-added marketing strategies, I want to make a very important point. Consistency over time creates results.

> *"People who say it cannot be done*
> *should not interrupt those who are doing it."*
> —Chinese Proverb

It is not savvy to do one video or podcast and expect significant results. Decide which three value-added marketing strategies you want to use and commit to being consistent in the creation and distribution of your expertise. Establish a regular schedule. Do you want to work on these strategies on a weekly, bi-weekly or monthly basis? You decide your time frame—just be consistent and trust that the significant results will come.

Deliver Successful Teleclasses

Remember that the key to attracting clients with ease is to provide valuable content before they become your client. Teleclasses create goodwill with current clients and allow you to introduce yourself to many new people at once without leaving your office.

Make sure you offer value-added content; your free teleclass should not be a sales pitch. However, make sure you include a special offer for listeners to work with you or invest in one of your products or service offerings. *Make your offer simple, compelling and urgent.*

A teleclass usually occurs one time; teleseminars or telecourses are often ongoing classes. Offer a free teleclass once per month or once per quarter—invite people from your list and others who you do not know. A 25- to 30-minute teleclass instead of an hour-long teleclass might get more people to show up. A 45-minute teleclass may get more people to sign up for your offer. The key is to promote this call in different places so that you will attract attendees and introduce your business to new people.

Sometimes, you get a greater response from people when you make things exclusive. You can offer a teleclass only for your VIP clients. For example, an image consultant might do a teleclass for her clients each season to discuss the latest trends. A life coach might do a special call for her clients each January to discuss goals for the upcoming year. Consider doing a call for your previous clients offering them some content-rich information you were not offering before. This ensures repeat business and will increase referrals.

After a live teleclass, send a link of the recording to everyone on your email list who missed the call. Always include the duration of the call so people can decide whether to listen to it. If you record content that is not exclusively for paying clients, post it on your website.

Another way to build your email list and find more clients is to be a guest speaker on a teleclass for another expert or an organization. Many associations host teleclasses for their members. You can offer a free teleclass to an organization to build your list, or you can charge a fee for your teleclass and share the revenue with the organization as a fundraiser for them.

Promote your teleclasses to your own email contacts list, on your website, in your e-newsletters and on your online social networking sites and blogs. Ask your clients to pass an email invitation on to others they think might be interested. List your teleclass on a variety of websites for free or for a small fee. Create a teleclass promotion listing on social networking sites, such as Facebook® or LinkedIn®, where you can add all of your events to your profile page and post them to groups that would be interested in your topic.

To determine your teleclass topic, do the following:

• Determine what expertise you have that you could provide to a group over the phone.

• Make a list of topics that you might like to offer as a value-added teleclass to your existing clients and/or past clients.

• Make a list of topics you could offer as a complimentary teleclass to build your list.

Prepare and Post Podcasts

Podcasts and teleclass recordings are both audio content. A podcast is usually shorter and there are no participants on the line. A podcast is you delivering a recorded audio message, whereas teleclasses are often conducted live and are recorded as they are delivered. Teleclasses have participants online; podcasts usually do not.

Podcasts are quick, easy ways to publish audio information and establish expertise. Your clients and potential clients can hear you and experience your personality. When you record a podcast, speak directly to your audience, begin to build and strengthen relationships and get your message out. You can use a podcast to share all kinds of information, such as newsletter content, teleconference calls, interviews with other experts for cross-marketing, and any other creative use you can think of. Podcasts deliver your message and expertise directly onto your potential clients' desktops and digital players.

Audio can be easier to produce than writing text. Some experts find it easier and faster to record an audio message than to sit and write. You simply record your podcast message and save it as an MP3 file. Then upload it to your website and announce its availability to your mailing list. A website visitor can listen online or download it to their computer, iPod® or MP3 player. You can create a routine where you produce and upload a new podcast on the same day each week so people are drawn to your website regularly.

You can record a podcast of any length for free by going to www.simplevoicebox.com, download it and post it on your site. By the way, SimpleVoiceBox™ is a complete voice messaging system with multiple voicemail boxes, greetings and levels. To edit your audio content, use Audacity, free software you can download at www.audacity.sourceforge.net/download.

Speak Up for Success

Public speaking is a highly effective way to attract clients and establish your expertise. It is like having an introductory phone call or an initial appointment with a room full of people all at once.

When your name is on the event flyer, and you are standing in front of an audience speaking on your area of expertise, people view you as a true expert on your topic. When potential clients perceive you are an expert, they are much more likely to do business with you.

You can use speaking to grow your business, market your products and services and expand your network with influential, powerful contacts. It will help you:

• **Create new opportunities.** Speaking gets you in front of groups of people you may not otherwise meet. This can expand your sphere of influence and provide a variety of opportunities.

• **Get more clients, contracts and commissions.** Speaking can be more cost effective than direct mail, networking or cold calling. The rate of return on the time investment to prepare and deliver a speech could be the smartest action you could take to generate business. With a strong delivery and a high content speech, you could get at least one new client and maybe a lot more, every time you speak. You also can sell your products, such as a book or CDs, at the back of the room for additional income.

- **Get increased visibility.** Often, when you speak to a group, the group publicizes the event. People who do not attend the event read the information about your business and may give you a call.

- **Stay in touch with the public and your industry.** Speaking keeps you in touch and keeps you on your toes. It allows you to discover what issues are of concern to the people in your audience, and it can also help polish the public perception of your profession.

- **Get perks, perks and more perks.** As a speaker, you may receive nothing from the group that hosts you. However, sometimes you come home with beautiful flowers, dinner certificates and even hotel stays. In addition, once you become well-known as a speaker, you can receive opportunities to speak on cruises, at fancy resorts, and at exotic destinations—all expenses paid!

Speaking is more than just showing up and talking to the audience. You need to do some research and prepare to give a successful speech. Find out everything you can about a group to make sure they are the right match for you. Use the following five points to see if an opportunity is right for you.

- **Find out who will be in the audience.** You want to speak to your ideal clients. If you are asked to speak to other groups, that is fine for your community service, but it does not help build your business. You need to be compensated in some way with money or an opportunity to market to potential clients.

- **How far will you have to travel to deliver the speech?** You need to take time away from your workday to present your speech. The presentation must benefit your business enough to merit at least a half-day away from your regular business.

• **What is the amount of time you want to talk?** However much time the program chair or your event contact offers you, ask for more. The more time people spend with you, the more they invest with you, the more time you have to share your expertise, impress them and encourage them to become a client. Forty-five minutes is the minimum. Ninety minutes is great. The more the better.

• **What else is happening at this meeting?** If a group's officers are being installed, if an association is having a silent auction, if the president of the national organization or the mayor is coming to speak to a group, that is not the right night for you to present. You want to be the whole meal: the appetizer, salad, main course *and dessert*—not just the dessert. Avoid speaking at a meeting where there are many other special activities going on. You do not want anything else going on that will take attention away from you and your business.

• **Make sure you can take a couple of minutes toward the end of your presentation to let the audience know about your offerings.** If you are not allowed to do this, I strongly suggest you decline the opportunity unless you are receiving a generous honorarium or fee. Sometimes, such as at large national conferences, you cannot present your offerings. However, you may still want to pursue these speaking opportunities because they offer significant visibility, credibility and the opportunity to connect with your ideal clients throughout the conference.

Take a moment now to list three topics around which you could create a speech and three possible places where you could deliver each topic.

Write Your Way to Success

Writing about your expertise is a highly effectively way to draw new clients and opportunities to you. All you have to do is sit down and write. Writing is a valuable marketing tool because people keep information. You may be called by potential clients weeks, months or even years after an article sees print because they kept the article you wrote. Write about the topics and issues that answer the challenges your potential clients have and watch your phone begin to ring. Next are a few tips for easily writing articles to build your business.

• **Pay attention to your clients.** Listen to the questions your clients ask and identify the issues they want addressed. What challenges are your clients having? What challenges are plaguing the industry? What innovations are you hearing about? These are all great things about which to write. Keep a list, and when you are ready to write, review it for ideas.

• **Start with quick tips.** Start by writing a helpful list of something you know about but your clients might not. I call these "quick tip sheets." A couple of examples are "Twenty Quick Tips to Organize Your Office" or "Ten Ways to Feel Better in Five Minutes."

• **Turn it into an article.** To turn a quick tip sheet into an article, write an explanation or an example beneath each quick tip. Add an opening paragraph that states what problem your article solves, then add a paragraph at the bottom that tells the reader to apply what they have read—and you have a completed article.

• **Add a benefit-focused title.** Do not try to be too clever with your titles. Just tell the reader what to expect from reading your article. "Secrets," "strategies" and "solutions" are all good words to include in a title. For example, "Seven Secrets to Look Ten Years Younger" or "Ten Often Overlooked Solutions for Saving Money."

• **Remember the resource box.** The most important part of the article is the resource box at the bottom where you say who you are, what you do and how people can contact you. Include a compelling reason for readers to connect with you. For example, have them go to your website to download a free copy of an e-book or listen to your podcast that has even more tips.

• **Edit it.** Have a professional editor review your articles once they are written. You want to be confident everything you send out is accurate.

• **Use articles over and over.** Once you write an article or a quick tip sheet, use it again. Post it to websites, send it to publications that might be interested in it, and forward to members of the media. Email it to current clients and potential clients with a cover letter that says, "In case you missed my article in [name of publication], here is a copy for you." Of course, post your articles on your website, post a link to those articles on your social networking sites and post all or part of your articles on your blog, depending on length.

Marketing your business and establishing your expertise go hand-in-hand. People want to do business with the best, and you can use teleclasses, podcasts, speaking and writing to tell the world you are the best. For starters, choose one of these four tools that you are not currently using, make it part of your marketing plan and watch your success soar.

CATERINA RANDO, MA, MCC
Business Strategist, Speaker, Publisher

To your thriving business!

(415) 668-4535
cat@attractclientswithease.com
www.attractclientswithease.com
www.caterinaspeaks.com
www.thrivebooks.com

Caterina Rando's mission is to show entrepreneurs how to build thriving businesses. She is a sought-after speaker, business strategist and author of the national bestseller, *Learn to Power Think,* from Chronicle Books. She is featured as a success expert in six other leading business books.

Since 1993, Caterina has been committed to helping entrepreneurs succeed. Through her Business Breakthrough Program, she and her team show entrepreneurs how to become recognized as experts, streamline operations and significantly grow revenue. Known for delivering interactive, high-energy and high-content programs, Caterina is an award-winning professional speaker and trainer. She has delivered customized programs for organizations throughout the United States and abroad.

Caterina is also the founder of Thrive Publishing™, a company that publishes multi-author books, including this book, for experts who speak.

Caterina holds a bachelor of science degree in organizational behavior and an master of arts degree in life transitions counseling psychology. She is a Certified Personal and Professional Coach (CPPC) and a Master Certified Coach (MCC), the highest designation awarded by the International Coaching Federation. She is also affiliated with Q-Metrics to deliver programs on Emotional Intelligence in the Workplace and to use the EQ assessment tool.

Taking Relationships
to Referrals to Profit
By Mike Coy, RFC, CPBS

"Insanity: Doing the same thing over and over again
and expecting a different result."
—Albert Einstein, German-American physicist,
Nobel Prize winner

*L*earning how to take relationships to referrals to profit is a skill set anyone can learn. Harnessing the power of word-of-mouth referral marketing starts by developing the ability to take relationships to referrals to profit. This ability takes you away from the selling insanity most people have been taught for so long, and instead guides you toward connecting to persons of interest. Referrals and new business come from connecting through relationships—not convincing—which is selling!

The journey to developing relationships begins by recognizing the distinct behavioral traits of the people you wish to do business with, partner with or simply socialize with. Learning how *they* wish to be treated, learning how *they* wish to be approached, learning how *they* wish to do business with you requires strong observational techniques and a set of learned behavioral skills. When you develop these skills, your business will reach a level of success and profitability you never thought possible.

Sales Training vs. Referral Marketing

Would you love to play more, work less and make more money doing it? Most people would answer, Yes! Yes! Yes! That is less likely to happen if you continue to use the traditional sales training process that teaches you to convince people by answering their objections and countering their reluctance to make a decision by giving them a reason to move forward. The problem with this technique is simple common sense: People do not like to be sold; they like to buy!

With referral marketing, however, you are not directly involved in the selling process—someone else is. In fact, you are not even in the room! There is no convincing, just connecting. There is no need to answer objections because someone else has already done that for you. When a trusted friend or someone of interest tells a friend or associate about you, your products and services, they are informing. When you do it, you are selling. That is a huge difference. So how do you do this? By educating and motivating your referral partners—that is the key to this transformation.

Let's look at an example of how I tell my clients to take a lead and turn it into a referral.

John, my friend, says, "Mike, call Mary and tell her I told you to call."

You are taught to jump at this lead, right? Don't do it! Instead, turn it into a *referral*. Say something like this:

"Thanks John. This contact is important for me. Would you please call Mary and tell her about me and my products and service? Please let her know to expect my call."

Do you see the difference? Simply educating and motivating your referral source turns this lead into a much stronger client referral for you! Now when I call Mary, she will not answer the phone and say, "Who are you? What company?" Instead, she will say, "Yes, Mike, John said to expect your call, and he raves about your work."

Just making this change will see your closing ratio explode.

Taking DISC® Training to Another Level

Many of you have taken a DISC-style assessment, so you know if you are a High D (Dominant) or Low C (Compliant) person, but what about the person with whom you are working?

In my *"Referrals…If Not Now…When?"* continuing education workshops, I take the DISC program to another level of understanding and recognition. Dr. Ivan Misner, founder of Business Network International (BNI), Inc., explains it this way: "It's not who you know…it's how well you know them." It is all about *them*. It is how *they* want to be treated. When you are speaking with someone, always remember to answer for them: WIIFM—What's In It For Me?

I have developed my own personal assessment worksheet that allows you to understand your specific behavior styles, both natural and adaptive. Your natural style is what you are. It is who you are. Being adaptive is how you survive. The more adaptive you are, the higher the façade in many cases. That is why many salespeople collaborate or partner with someone with a more natural style than their own. Being overly adaptive can wear you out!

Once armed with this information, you can take a huge step in taking relationships to referrals to profit and learning how to network with them.

Recognizing if the person with whom you want to do business or become a referral partner is fast-paced or slow-paced is important information. Recognizing if he or she has a task-oriented or people-oriented behavioral style is also valuable information. Why? It is all about that person, and how he or she wants to be treated.

For example, let's say a real estate agent is showing a house to a couple. The agent is talking about the crown molding, granite counter tops and the beautiful view from the back porch when the couple only wants to know how close the nearest schools are and where the closest grocery store is located. The agent is way off the mark in influencing this couple. This deal may never happen. Always remember, it is not about you; it is about *them*.

> *"Sometimes I wonder whether the world is being run by smart people who are putting us on or by imbeciles who really mean it."*
> —Mark Twain, American humorist

I have broken down my four behavioral styles as follows:

- GGs = Go Getters™ (18 percent of population)

- SBs = Social Butterfly™ (28 percent of population)

- CTs = Caretakers™ (40 percent of the population)

- ABs = All Business™ (14 percent of the population)

What This Information Tells You

In my workshops, I explain to participants how these styles work.

- **GGs and SBs:** Fast-paced styles that want to change the world.

- **CTs and ABs:** Slow-paced styles that want to adjust to the world. They are much more methodical in their process, make slower decisions and question more before they move forward.

- **GGs and ABs:** Task-oriented styles. They want results. They are looking to finish the deal in a strong, profitable manner.

- **SBs and CTs:** People-oriented styles. They are much more into the "is-it-fun" aspect of the deal. They like the social connection, with the business connection coming later.

You cannot "pounce on" or try to "sell" to CTs or ABs. Why? It is what they are expecting, and it is not appreciated. How will you get them to be a referral partner or customer of yours if you treat them in a way that is uncomfortable or unsettling to them? You won't! In contrast, you cannot get too methodical or caught up in the details when dealing with GGs or SBs. They will turn you off, and the deal will never be done. Furthermore, they will not become a customer or strong referral partner for you. Knowing this information before and during the sales process is crucial to your ultimate success. Treat people the way *they* want to be treated, not the way you want to be treated. The result will speak for itself.

The idea here is to find those six to eight strong referral partners who can help you grow and expand your business. You do the same for them. This means you do not need the 500 to 1,000 referral partners some experts teach you to have.

This is not a one-time, simple sale. This is about developing long-term referral partnerships that will give both of you many sales. Developing this course of action involves learning behavioral styles and making something positive happen because of this knowledge. This can help you avoid mistakes and produce a more effective result. If you will pay attention, you can guess someone's specific behavioral style and have a strong understanding of how he or she wants to be treated.

Example:

- **GGs:** Be direct. Match their GG-ness. Make sure there is something in it for them. There must be a direct result in getting the deal done.

- **SBs:** Make it fun. It has to be uplifting and positive. Address what they are thinking: Are you as "cool" as I am? Can we be friends?

- **ABs:** Cross the T's and dot the I's. Character and integrity are musts. Know that they are thinking: Why is this person approaching me? What do they want?

- **CTs:** Don't sell. Don't pounce. Don't push. Trust is a big factor. Developing the relationship is essential. Don't make wholesale changes either.

How to Quickly Recognize and Respond to Each Behavioral Style

- **GGs:** Direct too much

- **SBs:** Talk too much

- **CTs:** Agree too much

- **ABs:** Question too much

Pay attention to the handshake; It says more than "Hello." You can get valuable clues about a person's style just by his or her handshake. Here's how each style meets and greets:

- **GGs:** Firm grip, direct eye contact, usually give first and last name.

- **SBs:** Quadruple pump, casual "How are you" greeting, usually give just their first name.

- **CTs:** Clasp hand over hand or arm, usually will not say name, direct eye contact, casual "Good to see you" greeting typical of politicians.

• **ABs:** Short, firm handshake, then they step back with a do-not-invade-my-space stance. They are all business.

I am convinced that understanding someone's specific behavioral style will allow you the opportunity to treat that person the way they want to be treated. This is not just a business tool. This process can be used with people everywhere to enhance your relationships.

Here is a final referral marketing success strategy to help you take that last step toward turning relationships to referrals to profit. So much of what we do as professional business people revolves around being seen, our exposure to the customer, and the direct result of business happening or not happening. Often, we spend a tremendous amount of time working on our visibility, ignoring our credibility, and not bridging the gap to profitability! I have the solution: The V-C-P Success 101 Equation.

The V-C-P Success 101 Equation: It Will Change the Way You Do Business Forever!

My friend and mentor, Dr. Ivan Misner, the founder of BNI, Inc., is recognized as one of the top networking experts in the world. Several years ago, he taught me this V-C-P Success 101 Equation.

V-C-P stands for:

• Visibility

• Credibility

• Profitability

Most people spend 96 percent of their time on the Visibility factor, but that leaves only 4 percent of their time for Credibility and Profitability. They attend a networking mixer and go straight from

Visibility to Profitability and skip over Credibility entirely. Then they wonder why their networking efforts are not producing any business!

Why do people skip Credibility? Because the C factor takes the most time, but it is the most important factor for ultimate success. Eliminating the C factor prevents you from getting to the P factor, and without the P factor, your financial success is threatened.

How many times have you seen a sales professional approach a perfect stranger, introduce himself or herself, hand over a business card and ask for business? They go straight from the V factor to P—eliminating the C factor.

What if there were another way to look at this formula that ensured you would never skip over the C factor? If you concentrate on the P factor first, then C and finally V, your business would grow. How? Try this experiment: Go to an existing client who knows you, trusts you and with whom you have done business in the past. This client understands your product and service. That's the P factor. You have already made a profit from this person's business. The C factor—credibility—is also there. He or she knows you and trusts you and knows your product and service. Ask this person to approach three friends or associates for you using the technique from the beginning of this chapter. Your client will "inform," so you do not have to "sell." That's the correct way to sell using V-C-P.

Existing clients are the most overlooked group of referral sources you have. Allow your existing clients to help you grow and expand your business by connecting and taking your relationships to referrals to profit.

My motto is, "pursue the path of least resistance. Do business with those who benefit greatly from doing business with you."

The more you learn how to recognize how to take relationships to referrals to profit, the more you enhance your ability to be more confident in communicating what you do and why you are the person with whom to do business. You will have the education and sales training skill set to be successful, and these strong, referral-based, word-of-mouth marketing skills will move your business forward quickly and painlessly.

Although many traditional tools, such as advertising, public relations, websites, social media and cold calling are all valuable marketing resources, once you learn how to harness the power of word-of-mouth referral marketing, you will see an increase in sales and develop sustainable business growth. You will stop trying to convince people to buy your product or service and concentrate on connecting with them to build long-term relationships that will sustain you through good economic times, as well as tough economic times.

These strategies will give you an advantage so you can move higher and more quickly within your organization or up the ladder of success. More important, this knowledge will allow you to enjoy more self-confidence, the respect of your clients and peers and the genuine admiration of all you meet and lead. Knowledge alone is not power; what you do with knowledge is the power.

Educating and motivating your referral sources correctly will give you an opportunity to take your existing relationships to referrals to profit. Remember, it is all about them and how they want to be treated. The more you understand and the more you help them be the best they can be, the more success you will have. That concept is called "Givers Gain": The more you give the more you gain. Now that you know how to take relationships to referrals to profit, go do it!

MIKE COY, RFC, CPBS

Do business with those who benefit greatly from doing business with you

(512) 554-3778
mcoy@austin.rr.com
www.referraltrainingcenters.com

Mike is based in Austin, Texas, where he serves a diverse audience of clients including professional sales executives, real estate agents, CPAs, Group 1 insurance agents, financial planners and others who want to learn how to harness the power of word-of-mouth referral marketing. For more than thirty years, he has guided professionals to proactively increase their business by implementing a structured referral marketing strategy through the *Referrals...If Not Now... When?*™ continuing education training programs. These programs are a proven path to success and increased profits.

Mike's signature three-hour workshop, *Taking Relationships to Referrals to Profit,* has educated and motivated thousands of sales professionals across the United States. Mike is a Registered Financial Consultant and a Master DiSC® Certified Professional Behavior Specialist.

Mike is a sought-after public speaker with his various referral marketing workshops and motivational talks. He is a past president of the Austin Westlake Chamber of Commerce and past publisher of *Broker Agent Magazine* of Central Texas. As one of the top referral marketing gurus in the nation, Mike's energetic, engaging manner makes his presentations educational, motivational, informative and fun!

Developing an Incredible Business Network
By Darlene Willman

"The richest people in the world look for and build networks, everyone else looks for work."
—Robert T. Kiyosaki, American investor and author

*E*stablishing a professional network is the foundation of all wealth. Whoever you are, whatever you do, the people in your network can add priceless value to your business.

Make a commitment to grow your network every day. Find a place you can interact with others and get to know all about them. If you belong to a club or organization, try to find one that allows for open discussions and socializing.

Some networking groups are too structured and do not give you much time to interact. Look for specific groups that have the people in them whom you want to meet, and the ability to actually network with them.

Get to know people by spending time with them either on the phone or in person. Better yet, try to get to know them online too! Find out where they hang out and plug into their network.

If you have not already set up your profile online with some social networks, I highly recommend you do it soon. The Internet is the best network that was ever created. For more on building your network online, see Karen Clark's chapter on *Online Social Networking for Business* on page 213.

Set a goal to attend one function each week and meet at least ten new people at each event. If you multiply that by 52 weeks, you have now added over 500 people to your network in a year. What about finding 10 new people with whom to network online each week, too? Now you've added over a thousand people in one year.

Always be looking at how you can add quality connections to your network each week. I make it a point to attend conferences, trade shows, workshops and seminars where I meet other like-minded people. I'm not interested in just adding a name to my list, but in finding a strong, dynamic individual to whom I can relate and who understands me.

People are meeting everywhere from social gatherings to structured business networking. If you are just beginning to network, I would suggest joining a local Business Network International (BNI, Inc.) group where you will meet with the same people each week and send referrals to only those in your group.

There are also civic groups and nonprofit organizations that have meetings to discuss their plans or the current projects on which they are working. One of my favorite places to network is at a charity event where I not only support a great cause, but I can meet some of the most generous people in our community.

If you are adventurous and have time to invest, you might consider belonging to a board where you can contribute your area of expertise or lend a helping hand. Volunteering can be a very effective way of getting involved and easily increasing your network. I would also caution you to not join too many, at least not in the beginning.

Women especially tend to volunteer more sometimes because they are natural caregivers. Unfortunately, if you give all your time away for free, you will not be generating a solid income for your new business. Carefully select what you want to be involved in before making any commitments.

Another great way to increase your contacts is speaking to a group that consists of your target audience. When you are the speaker, you are positioned as the expert and people will automatically want to get to know you—that is, if you give a great presentation. For more on public speaking to grow your business, see Caterina Rando's chapter on *How to Be Recognized as an Expert and Attract Clients with Ease* on page 179.

Developing your network should be a part of your marketing plan. Create a plan that you can implement easily and effortlessly. Remember, your network is your most valuable asset!

Before You Go Networking, Have a Game Plan

When you prepare for success, you will attract success. It is so important to take time prior to attending a networking function to think about a few important things.

First, where are you going? If you are new to networking or just starting your business, you might want to try a variety of networking meetings before committing to them on a regular basis. I would suggest attending no more than three events per week and no less than one per week.

After you have determined the networks in which you want to participate and build, mark them on your calendar every month until the end of the year. Networking only works when you make a full commitment to being present each month. Those who "show up" usually reap the rewards of gaining referrals. Networking is an important part of your marketing plan. Make sure to follow through to be seen as dependable.

Decide if you would like to go with someone or by yourself. Some people find comfort in attending functions with someone who I call your "networking buddy." This way, you can be a team and not have the fear of being left alone. Whether you plan on meeting in advance to drive together or simply meet there, make a quick phone call to confirm your arrangement.

Visualize yourself meeting many interesting people and attracting the right referral partners into your life. You might meet someone who is immediately interested in what you offer. Keep in mind, though, that few people do business when they first meet someone.

Practice your 60-second introduction over and over until you feel confident in saying it to several people. Write it out and repeat it to yourself or share it with your networking buddy. Make sure to include your name, company name, the typical problem most of your customers have and how you can provide a solution—plus a call to action. A call to action simply means an action step you want your audience to take. A few examples would be, "call today for a free quote," "visit our website at xyz.com," or "if you'd like a free report please hand me your business card and I'll send it to you."

A few important things to bring with you include business cards, a pen, some free promotional items or other leave-behind pieces such as brochures, postcards or flyers. You will not be passing these items out to everyone unless they specifically ask for them. Don't assume that everyone wants information about what you offer.

Set a goal to meet five new connectors or referral partners at the event. Maybe look for other people who have a target audience similar to yours and see about collaborating on a project. Listen to announcements of what additional events are coming up that you might want to attend. If you have been attending the same event for several months, maybe try to schedule three on-the-spot appointments or schedule lunch or coffee with someone new. Make sure to bring your calendar for the upcoming week.

Before walking out the door, freshen up, take some breath mints (just in case), check your attitude and don't forget to smile when you get there!

Your Approachability Factor

Think for a minute, on a scale from one to ten, how approachable do you think you are? Almost everyone thinks they are extremely approachable and would rate themselves at the high end. I bet you said you're at least an eight if not a ten! Unfortunately, other people may have a different opinion.

How we present ourselves in public depends on how we hold our posture, our manners, our persona and our body language. For example, if you are at a function and standing near the doorway or the back of the room, you actually communicate that you will be exiting if the environment does not hold your interest. Perhaps you have another engagement and need to leave early. That's completely understandable, and the rest of the room may interpret that differently.

Another way of communicating by how you stand is having your arms crossed. You might fidget a lot and may not know what to do with your hands, or maybe you think it is more comfortable for you to fold your arms across your chest. However, this can be interpreted as being closed off to anyone's approach. It can also suggest skepticism and doubt. This might say, "Prove it to me" or be seen as a power stance or dominating.

The direction of your eyes also suggests when you are engaged in conversation or if you are thinking of something else. If you avoid eye contact altogether, you will not be approached by very many people at the event. People are looking for trust in networking relationships, and direct eye contact builds trust.

Avoid carrying things or occupying both hands, as it is difficult for someone to shake your hand and introduce themselves if your hands are full. Ladies, find a way to either carry things in a bag over your shoulder or at least leave your right hand free to shake. This also applies when you have a plate in your hand and a drink. Usually, you are preoccupied with eating instead of connecting. Consider eating prior to attending if possible or eat when the meeting starts. Reserve the time at the beginning of the event to just mingle and you'll be more approachable.

Of course, the final sign that signals you're available to talk with someone is to offer a bright and cheerful smile to someone and simply say, "Hello." Be the one who makes the initial contact and engages in conversation.

Networking the Room

When you invest your time, money and resources into networking, you will want to make the most of your experience. Often people show up at an event just to socialize and eat, expecting other people to do all the work. Just showing up doesn't always mean you'll get the business.

The word "work" is in the middle of networking, implying you have to put forth effort to get results. Some people do it for fun or are addicted to the social side of networking. Unfortunately, just schmoozing doesn't lead to business.

Before you attend, think of who might be there. A chamber of commerce event will have mostly business owners and community leaders. If it is an association or civic group, you might meet people who volunteer and so on. Do not assume you will meet everyone who attends, so be realistic with the number of people with whom you want to connect.

Briefly, say hello to people you already know, but do not talk too long. You can always meet with them on another occasion to catch up. Your goal is to meet new people and if you spend too much time with people you already know, you'll miss out on an important introduction.

You can meet at least ten new people in one hour or less, so keep your conversations to no more than three to five minutes long. If you noticed you have been with the same person for more than ten minutes, you should excuse yourself politely and move on. Tell them it was great meeting them and you hope to see them again soon.

Here are a few simple ways you can network the room:

• Greet people with a smile and a handshake.

• Maintain eye contact with them.

• Spend only a few minutes with each person.

• Ask open-ended questions.

• Ask them to introduce you to someone they know there.

• If you see someone else you know, introduce the person with whom you are speaking to him or her.

- Interact with as many people as possible.

- Be approachable.

- Eat last or skip it altogether; you can't talk with a mouth full of food!

- Avoid sitting at a table with people you know.

- Decide up front if you want to sit with a variety of business owners or one group. For example, most people who work for a particular company or government agency often stay clustered together.

- Be the leader or facilitator at your table.

- Be on the welcoming committee and meet all the guests.

Anytime you offer assistance, you are creating a sense of trust and being resourceful. Both of these are critical in building professional relationships.

It is not a contest where you are competing with people to get the most business cards. It is about spending your time wisely and efficiently. Try not to rush through people as if you are on a mission. Be sincere and polite to each person you meet. Remember, first impressions will last forever—so be professional.

Visualize a hummingbird that goes from flower to flower—you will hear them buzzing. They visit each flower for only a few short seconds, extracting the essence of what they are after. Be specific about what you're after, whether that's a prospect, an introduction or simply to exchange business cards.

If you meet ten new people, you will need to follow up with those ten people after the event. Consider the number of events you will attend each week and determine how full you want your calendar.

The more you attend, the more people you will meet, the more follow-up and time involved.

Five Easy Follow-Up Steps You Should Take After You Network

The key to establishing a strong network is to include ways to stay connected and be involved with the other person. More than eighty percent will fail to follow up and miss out on potential business opportunities.

Follow these five easy steps:

1. Send a quick email to everyone with whom you connected, letting them know how much you enjoyed meeting them. Include all your contact info. However, avoid sending sales material and do not ask them to buy anything. Instead, ask them to reply to the email with what makes a great referral for them and keep it for future reference.

2. Send them a LinkedIn® request so you always know what company they are with and stay up to date. This will also give you web-based access to their contact info so you can find them any time you can get online.

3. Become their friend on Facebook® and learn as much as you can about them while sharing more about yourself. The easiest way to build a relationship is by giving information to each other and opening the lines of communication.

4. Enter their contact info into your contact management system and store their information in a safe place. At the same time, send them a quick card in the mail with your contact info in case they want to call you.

5. If you think you have potential business to talk about, pick up the phone and call them for an appointment. Consider scheduling a quick meeting for coffee or lunch to discuss possible resources or connections you might have to give them.

Do not assume your network will keep up with you and what you offer; that is up to you. How you follow up and keep up with *them* is what makes the difference between you getting their business or losing them to your competition.

Although you will not always have a lot of time to do everything, at least do these steps immediately after you meet someone, ideally within the first 24 to 48 hours. The longer you wait, the harder it is for your new contacts to recall where they met you and why they need to get to know you better. Begin to follow the advice in this chapter, and soon you will find that you have built an incredible network.

DARLENE WILLMAN
ACCOMPLISH™ Magazine & Radio
U.S. Small Business Conference

Improve Your Mindset, Skillset & Network

(636) 387-3000
info@darlenewillman.com
www.accomplishmagazine.com
www.ussmallbusinessconference.com

Darlene Willman is dedicated to supporting small businesses by sharing resources, connections, knowledge and services locally and across the nation. Having organized over 100 professional networking events in her career and spoken to a variety of audiences, she is a predominant leader in her field.

Darlene is featured in The Networking Masters Program along with Dr. Ivan Misner, founder of Business Network International, Bob Burg, author of *Endless Referrals,* published by McGraw-Hill in 2005, and many others. She has written and published over 100 articles on networking and business best practices. She received the 2008 award from the U.S. Small Business Administration for *Women in Business Champion of the Year*, was nominated for *Most Influential Business Women* in St. Louis and the *First Lady Award for Business and Innovation*. Darlene is the CEO and founder of the U.S. Small Business Conference. Her recent achievements include the publishing of *Accomplish Magazine.*

As a successful, tech savvy multipreneur, wife and mother, Darlene has a well-established network with professionals from all around the world. When she's not networking in person, you can find her online at Facebook®, LinkedIn® and Twitter® or at darlenewillman.com.

Online Social Networking for Business
Strategies for Building an Online Presence
By Karen Clark

"Social media tools are modern day galleons that will carry you to the new world, allowing you to share your passion, differentiate yourself from your competitors, and deliver your brand to the broadest possible audience."
—Gary Vaynerchuk, American businessman,
author and television producer

When I first began marketing my business online in 1998, I really had no idea what to expect. Setting up a website was time-consuming and tedious, especially since I had to figure out what I was doing along the way. Something told me that the Internet would be the key to expanding my reach—and I was right. Our family had just been transferred from one corner of the country to the other, and I was looking for a way to keep my business going despite the move. Creating and promoting my website turned out to be the best thing I did for my business because of the connections I was making with people online. The world became smaller, and this allowed me to make a difference for people who wanted to hear my message and who would benefit from my product.

What Is Online Social Networking and Why Do I Need It?

You may have a thriving business already, or your calendar may already be full, and you may be wondering why you should get involved in online social networking. The fact is that in this era, you cannot afford not to! More and more businesses are setting up profiles on social media sites, participating in conversations, and attracting new clients and customers online. When a business does not use online social networking, customers and clients find those who do and interact with them instead.

According to econsultancy.com, as of early 2010, there were more than 350 million people using Facebook®, over 75 million people using Twitter®, and over 50 million people using LinkedIn®. The rate of increase in these statistics over a six-month period in 2009 was astounding—active social media users increased by 40 percent. It is still growing! Facebook recently broke the 500 million mark.

Participating in social media is no longer an activity reserved for the youth. In fact, www.insidefacebook.com reports that the largest growing demographic for Facebook users is women over the age of 55. As online social networking becomes more and more mainstream, opportunities for businesses to expand their reach are increasing to the point of it now being a vital part of their marketing plans.

Participating in online social networking is an affordable and effective way to meet the exact people who are looking for the services or products your business offers. Using the power of search engines to establish an online presence, businesses can attract attention to themselves simply by providing fresh, relevant, useful content anywhere they choose. The most common social networking venues in which businesses can participate are Facebook, Twitter, LinkedIn, YouTube, and Yelp. Whether you have a regular website or not, conducting business through these social media platforms allows you to build a positive reputation and increase your expert status while bringing in new business with a minimal investment.

It's About Networking

Think of social media sites as a different form of "real life" networking. Many of us attend business meetings, chamber events, and referral clubs in hopes of meeting new clients. Of the guests at these events, some will be very interested in finding out more about who we are, some will be mildly curious and may send a referral our way, and others will simply not be a match for us. We understand this and show up hoping we will go home with some new business. Participating in networking and community events is a proven method for reaching new people because the focus is on making meaningful connections with those whose needs we can serve. For more on networking information, see the previous chapter *Developing an Incredible Business Network* by Darlene Willman on page 201.

The same is true for online social networking. It is another way of meeting new people who can be a source of revenue for your business. Just like in-person networking events, in order to benefit, you have to show up consistently, participate enthusiastically and follow up with some personal contact. Those who have been able to see the parallels between the two types of networking are the businesses that have been able to translate their social media efforts into solid results.

Go Where They Gather

One of the most effective ways to market yourself online through social networking is by positioning yourself in the conversations of people in your targeted market. Just as you would find a specific market to serve in your area and participate in business and community events, the same goes for online social networking. In the online world, you can target your efforts by finding similar communities through the social networks. Create a profile that includes a short bio and a professional headshot, participate in discussions, comment on articles and blog posts, share your own ideas and opinions, and, generally, make yourself well known as someone with whom people would want to do business. Following are some popular communities to join.

LinkedIn Groups—www.linkedin.com/groupsdirectory. LinkedIn has quite an extensive network of social groups to join. Search by category or by geographic location to find people who might be interested in your expertise. Posting discussion questions and answering questions that members pose to the group is a great way to get involved and build your reputation among LinkedIn users. When you publish a blog post or find a useful article online, you can also post the links to the News tab of the group, further enhancing your presence in the group.

Ning Communities—www.ning.com. Use the search box to find groups that are related to a specific keyword, such as "entrepreneur" or "business women." By joining the Ning groups with the highest numbers of members and with the best quality content posted, you are more likely to connect with people who are looking for your product or services. Utilize the built-in features, such as discussion groups, video sharing and blog posts.

Hashtags on Twitter—www.tweetchat.com. Using hashtags (the practice of appending a # key to the beginning of a keyword or abbreviation and including it in a tweet), is a way for Twitter users to track group discussions, community gatherings, or live chat topics. Tweetchat is a straightforward way to participate in conversations around a certain topic by automatically inserting the hashtag in your posts and allowing you to follow the discussion in real time. Typically, hashtag users assume that others who use the hashtag are interested in similar topics to them and will often follow others in the group. For example, following the hashtag #GNO on Tweetchat is a way to participate in a Girls' Night Out discussion for women. Find new hashtags to follow at www.hashtags.org.

Regardless of the online social networking group in which you participate, make sure you are aware of the protocol within the group. Above all, focus on how you can contribute to meaningful conversation and build relationships with the members.

Going Local Online

What if your particular business only serves local, in-person clients? What can you do to reach out to people in your own backyard? It used to be that consumers consulted a large, printed book of yellow pages when they needed to find a photographer, bookkeeper or real estate agent. If they were not sure where to go for art supplies, books or pizza, they let their fingers do the walking. The majority of today's consumers, however, turn to online searches and directories to find what they are looking for. Within a few seconds, they get information about the closest service provider, restaurant or shop with real-time customer reviews, ratings and "buzz" that influences their decision on which businesses to patronize.

Making sure that your business shows up in the search results is determined by whether or not you have your town, county, or region listed on your website, blog, or social media profiles, and if you have a presence on several of the online social networks that serve a local clientele. Here are some of the most popular and higher-ranking sites.

Yelp—biz.yelp.com. Yelp is the most popular business rating, feedback and referral social network. Because of its popularity, when your business is listed, you have a powerful presence on the web. Past customers and clients can write reviews and testimonials on your business profile, and potential new customers can find you, learn more about your business, and contact you.

Merchant Circle—www.merchantcircle.com. This network allows businesses to create mini-websites, blogs, coupons and newsletters–free. Consumers for whom it is important to use local business, instead of chain stores or franchises, appreciate being able to depend on Merchant Circle to steer them toward truly local, responsive companies who offer them incentives to do business with them.

Yahoo®, Google® and Bing™ LOCAL—local.yahoo.com, local. google.com, local.bing.com. Each of these three major search engines has local business listings where you can create a complete profile for your business. Customers can rate your service, leave a review or testimonial, and share your profile with their contacts. Your profile shows up toward the top of the results when someone local searches for one of your products, services or keywords.

The New ROI: Return on Interaction

Measuring your return on investment in business is a standard practice for any business owner or entrepreneur who wants to become and stay profitable. Knowing the specific monetary results that come from your investments of time and money guides your business decisions. When it comes to online social networking, however, there are gray areas that often make people uncomfortable. Business owners are wondering where the return is. When is this going to pay off? Most of all, is this worth my time and money when I have other measurable marketing strategies I can use?

With online social networking, the return is not on the investment; the return is on the interaction. You do not put in money to get more money—you put in interaction to get more interaction, which returns tenfold in trust, loyalty and the development of advocates for your business. The result is an increased number of email newsletter subscriptions, Twitter followers, Facebook fans or blog comments. From there, you can typically track an increase in the number of product orders, new clients or referrals.

Here are some resources that can help you get the most return on your interactions online.

Google Analytics—www.google.com/analytics. Google Analytics is the big daddy of online measurement, especially when it comes to a traditional website's ranking in the search engines. You can now access analytics on many of your social networking profiles by tracking their URLs. Google Analytics will measure inbound links as well as some of what the visitors to your profile searched before finding you, and where they go when they leave.

Grader.com—www.grader.com. Grader offers various tools for evaluating and making suggestions to increase your online presence. Based on a scale of 1 to 100, you will be given a grade that takes into account the number of fans, followers or subscribers you have, how often you post and the number of times someone has passed your postings on to their contacts.

Hootsuite—www.hootsuite.com. Hootsuite allows you to participate in, monitor and analyze accounts from several platforms including Facebook profiles and fan pages, Twitter and LinkedIn from one website. It also can schedule your non-conversational posts in advance, which can be a timesaver when you have something to broadcast or will be away from the office. It includes automatic URL, photo, and file sharing options that can be tracked. This gives you useful data about who is taking action or sharing.

Netiquette—Social Media Manners

When it comes to minding your manners, nowhere online are the benefits more abundant and the consequences more swift than through social networking. Following protocol, which varies among the different programs, is vital, and sometimes your innocent mistakes or the errors of those to whom you are connected can repel your readers, and at worst, get you kicked off the network.

The good news is that there are really only five rules to follow that cover almost every situation.

1. Remember the Golden Rule. Treat others the way you would like to be treated. We grow up hearing this, but when it comes to online social networking, many business owners forget that. Be courteous, kind, honest, and respectful of your customers and readers. Offer a superior service or product that will benefit their lives and promote them in a respectful and courteous manner.

2. Speak when spoken to. Customers today want to know that a live person is behind the social media profile. Check your Facebook fan page for comments and reply, answer your @ replies on Twitter, and engage in conversation through your blog comments. There is nothing worse for your online presence than customer feedback or questions going unanswered publicly.

3. Honesty is the best policy. Be forthcoming and honest with your customers whenever possible. Being up front about delays or changes builds trust and loyalty. Manipulating your customers and using marketing tricks to increase your numbers does not work. To gain quality, targeted customers who are loyal to you, be transparent.

4. Measure twice. Cut once. While we are being honest, interactive and respectful, we also need to maintain a positive professional image online. Be sure you present yourself and your business with the exact image you want to convey. Proofread or spell check your responses and check writing conventions, tone and voice. Filter out posts that are too heavily opinionated or that risk alienating certain demographics.

5. Your word is your bond. Your customers and potential customers have, at some point, been let down by businesses or organizations, and if you let them down, they will simply choose another business to patronize. When starting to participate in online relationships, do what you say you will do when you say you will do it. Keep agreements with your readers and follow through on requests. Appearing flaky even for a moment will result in losing your customer to someone else.

Standing Above the Rest

Any business can create a social networking presence. The tools are at your disposal, instructions are readily available, and access to the vast world online is relatively easy. Not every business will do this, but you can create a true presence that results in champions and advocates who will spontaneously engage their own networks to share a great resource—you! In order to turn contacts into online champions, start today to:

• Go where they gather. Choose one new place to hang out with your potential customers and participate.

• Focus on the interactions, the conversations and the level of engagement around your online social networks. That is where the real champions for your business are developed.

• Create an offline local presence on the online local directories. Welcome reviews, offer deals and thrive in your neighborhood.

- Apply the Golden Rule to every action you take online. Ask yourself, is this something I would do, be, or say in the offline world?

- Remember, people are at the heart of it all. Serve them well, and you will be served by them!

Get started on using the resources and strategies shared here, and soon your online presence will be strong and your new clients many.

KAREN CLARK
My Business Presence

An online presence training company

(707) 588-9290
karen@mybusinesspresence.com
www.mybusinesspresence.com

Karen Clark helps businesses improve their online presence through practical presentations, fun and effective workshops and webinars, and private consultations. She has 12 years of experience marketing online and is a co-author of *Direct Selling Power,* providing advice for building an online presence. She received Story Time Felts' Star Gazer Award for bringing innovative Internet marketing strategies to the field and has been successfully training others and implementing those strategies since 1998.

Karen is a chapter president and the California area coordinator of the Direct Selling Women's Alliance (DSWA), and she was honored with both their Spirit Award and their Ambassador of the Year Award. She regularly speaks to DSWA audiences about online presence and is featured in their *Mentored by the Masters* CDs. Karen also runs the North Bay Webify Your Business Club, which supports local small business owners in their online presence efforts through interactive weekly meetings.

Karen enjoys teaching others where, when and how to spend their time online to establish an effective online presence. Her positive, passionate and engaging manner and her ability to meet people where they are make her trainings informative and fun!

The Trade Show Phenomenon and How You Can Use It

By Marsha Reeves Jews

The 21st century has brought about an extraordinary number of marketing options for your business. The number of Internet advertising outlets range from social media to Google® ads on websites to annoying pop-ups. The maze of advertising overload is daunting, and it is difficult to move through cyberspace without touching someone's advertising campaign or creating a personal relationship with the customer.

As you navigate this fascinating journey of identifying the best complement of marketing outlets, the main ingredient for most businesses is the cost per unit. No matter where those valuable marketing dollars are spent, the bottom line is the bottom line. How do you get the best return on investment (ROI)?

Think Trade Shows!

Does your marketing strategy include trade shows? If it doesn't, it is certainly something to consider. This is one vehicle that gives you and your company an extraordinary direct marketing opportunity that can be supported by each of the other electronic and print media options you are considering.

There are several reasons why the tradeshow industry has grown exponentially over the last 30 years. Corporations have identified this medium as one of the leading opportunities to maximize their ROI, their company's profile and closing deals. Even if your business is small or you are an entrepreneur, you can also use this marketing segment to your advantage.

Having spent over twenty years developing, managing and marketing trade shows, expositions and conferences, I have learned that many buyers continue to focus on personal contact and relationship building. Many leaders believe it is often easier to do business with someone you know and can trust to service your business professionally.

The trade show circuit provides access to key decision makers and other influential members of their team. There is absolutely nothing like being face to face with your clients and prospects, armed with all your marketing materials and a stellar sales force.

What is interesting about this industry is that during these annual events you continuously connect with your clients or prospects. It is comforting to walk into a room or trade show hall and see familiar faces. These impromptu opportunities create the ability either to develop or build relationships. Make certain these meetings end in inviting your new-found friend to your booth, setting an appointment to meet or pitching your company and product.

What Is A Trade Show?

A trade show is a marketplace where companies from an array of industries showcase their products, services, developers, marketing team and corporate marketing information. They are usually held in a hotel lobby, convention center or exhibit hall and last about six to eight hours a day, for one to three days. The common goal is to meet with current customers and/or potential buyers and have them purchase your products or services. It is like a farmers' market where each farmer has a booth or table and, throughout the day, they try to entice people to purchase their produce.

Trade shows are direct marketing opportunities to present your product or services in venues where associations, conferences or independent trade show producers bring together buyers and sellers for a specific target market. You will find corporate, retail, public buyers and key leaders discussing their mutual needs and benefits up close and personal. Some trade shows are connected with a specific industry conference or convention and often include social functions and seminars.

An interesting aspect to this industry is that they can have direct or indirect, horizontal or vertical relationships to your industry. For example, the American Bar Association would be a great place to present software, temporary services, furniture and other products that support that particular industry.

Which Trade Show Is Right for You?

There is generally a trade show that supports your specific business sector through a national or local trade association. Whether it is medical, legal, manufacturing, retail clothing industry or high tech, a trade show exists.

Start with research, more research, and even more research. Identify the trade show that matches your market segment. You can contact the appropriate trade associations, check online under trade shows and go to the library or bookstore to review the trade magazines that usually have advertisements announcing upcoming trade shows. I recommend you contact the trade show management. These folks want your business, can answer whatever questions you may have and assist you in making the decision to participate.

Ask about past participants and their demographics. Identify which sponsors have attended; who the speakers and honorees were and their respective industries; request attendance numbers for the last several years; ask for names of companies and a contact for references.

It is important to speak with past participants to obtain a better understanding of how the trade show traffic flows, confirm attendance numbers and learn about the ancillary activities to help you plan staff, materials and potential marketing opportunities. There is nothing better than to speak with someone who has had a direct experience at a trade show, particularly a sponsor.

It is also a great investment to actually attend the trade shows you are considering. Prior to committing to a booth, many companies will send their representatives to monitor attendance, gauge the caliber of attendees and participate in social activities.

To aid you in your marketing planning, ask about each trade show's marketing strategy. How do they plan to attract your client base, and how can you maximize your visibility through their marketing campaign?

What Can You Expect?

The marketing materials you receive will include valuable exhibitor information and pricing for the exhibit space, floor plans, shipping information, contracts, audio-visual equipment, furniture rental, signage, sponsorship, advertising opportunities, hotel and registration information.

You can purchase exhibit spaces in a number of sizes, varying between 60 and 100 square feet. You can also purchase additional booth space in 60 to 100 square-foot increments to expand your presence. Your investment generally includes a six-foot table, two chairs, wastebasket, side drapes and a small 24 x 44-inch sign for your company name and booth number.

There is usually a magazine or trade show program that will automatically list your company as an exhibitor and include a copy of the exhibit hall floor plan with your booth number and company name. Additionally, you may want to take advantage of the opportunity to participate as a sponsor or purchase advertising space to extend your marketing message.

Many trade shows connected to an association or convention will have social functions that may or may not be included in your level of participation. Here is an opportunity to enhance your visibility. If this is your first time participating in a particular trade show, attend the featured event. These social events are excellent marketing opportunities. While sponsorship opportunities are a great way to gain visibility, they can be expensive. You might want to consider having a specialty item with your logo and contact information placed inside the tote bags that are given to attendees. However, if your budget allows, there are numerous marketing opportunities that could also be suggested to the trade show managers. For example, placing your name on the hotel key cards; sponsoring travel or a hotel room for a speaker; defraying some of the cost for tote bags, name tag holders, posters or t-shirts; becoming a sponsor or co-sponsor for a welcome reception; sponsoring a table or bus to transport speakers.

During this three- or four-day period, waves of people will move through the exhibit hall throughout the day. Attendance is often dependent upon whether or not there are concurrent seminars or workshops during exhibit hours. Review the entire schedule of events and find out when you can expect peak activity in the exhibit hall. This will help in your scheduling of pertinent staff.

If yours is a small or mid-size business, it may be difficult to send additional employees to manage your booth. This is a great opportunity to contact a temporary agency in the host city for assistance. However, it is very important for you to schedule a training session so the individual(s) can thoroughly understand your product or services. Should your budget allow, bring your seasoned team. This would be an opportunity to "divide and conquer." You could easily send a sales rep, armed with business cards that include your booth number, to several strategic seminars and workshops where they would have the opportunity to meet and schmooze with potential clients. Meanwhile, your booth is being managed by other well-trained team members.

Don't be concerned that you are a small business or entrepreneur; you can manage and take advantage of this marketing opportunity. This is where your creativity comes into play.

A small business client was trying to determine whether to participate in an upcoming trade show that was part of a small business conference for the state of Maryland, and was a little nervous about how she could manage participating. The biggest issues were whether she could host her booth without staffing and also afford the production of collateral materials.

We determined that the company could be represented with a couple of family members who knew her business and could learn the sales script. She made a small investment with a local art student who created an image that was blown up for her reusable backdrop. This same image was used on an oversized postcard, a DVD and a video of her products in use, all of which were a big hit. The innovative addition of a raffle drawing for dinner for two was a barter deal with a local restaurant.

The end result: She received more business card contacts than she could have met in a month and had the opportunity to discuss sub-contracting opportunities with the leadership of the state of Maryland. Even if your business is small, you can participate in large trade shows if you are creative, determined and focused on the bottom line.

How to Maximize Your ROI

It is now time to execute your strategic marketing plan and best strategic thinking skills. Remember, investing in attending a trade show is all about the mission; to take home orders for your products or services.

When participating in trade shows, you are deploying a comprehensive tactical marketing plan by pre-marketing, on-site marketing and post-event marketing. These three phases can enhance your visibility and create an air of excitement for your product or services through an integrated message and a plan of action for advertising, direct sales, public relations and communication. All are critical for your overall success.

- **Pre-marketing.** Announcing your participation, sending invitations to a special event or to visit your booth, advertising in industry journals and on your website

- **On-site marketing.** Exhibit design and message, trained sales force, collateral material and incentives

- **Post-event marketing.** Immediate follow-up with clients or prospects; press releases, direct mail and telephone contact

Your Booth Can Make or Break You

Once you have identified the appropriate tradeshow and received information, act swiftly to decide your booth location. The most prominent and desirable space is closest to the entrance on a corner of the main aisle.

In many cases, larger booths will take advantage of these corner locations. If this space is not available, look for locations that are about two to three spaces into the center of the adjacent aisle on the right side off the main entrance aisle. Having observed the behavior of many attendees walking through exhibit halls, I have found it interesting how they tend to focus on companies that are near the entrance or just off the main aisles.

What can you do in your booth that is exciting, innovative, creative and memorable? What could you include in your booth that will attract the attendees to you and not your competitor?

Imagine walking into an exhibit hall and seeing a large logo, hearing music or smelling freshly-brewed coffee. Your curiosity takes over; your immediate thought is to find out what is going on. Make sure it is your booth they visit first by including something to pique their interest and draw them to your booth, such as sound, video monitors, balloons, or an interactive game.

The design of your booth, materials and personnel are all a reflection of your brand. As you begin to conceptualize your collateral materials, it is critical that your materials and signage have a consistent message and a visual relationship to one another. Think sound bites. As attendees walk down your aisle, they read tons of verbiage; your message has to tell your story and resonate with their needs while luring them to your booth.

Depending on the size of your booth, invest in a professionally designed and manufactured portable display. You can find them in a variety of prices, dimensions, sizes and styles, such as tabletop, double panels, floor models and so on. These displays can be folded into containers with wheels and checked at the airport, eliminating shipping charges. You can also purchase the larger, more expensive displays that have multiple panels, space for monitors, counters and cardholders for your marketing materials. These can be shipped and delivered to your booth.

Consider having actual products or videos that demonstrate your product in action, show people using the product or giving testimonials. Putting them on a loop is highly effective and recommended. This provides uninterrupted time for the client to learn about your product or services, consider how they could use them and develop questions.

Preparing to Staff Your Booth

Staff training is essential. You want prepared or experienced people to work your booth. You can have the best product or services in the world; however, it can be lost on the prospect without the vital contribution of your booth staff. They will determine whether you can close the sale with a potential customer.

Develop a standard protocol in the booth: how to properly approach the customer with the right sales pitch, the appropriate decorum and demeanor. A prospect will take three to five minutes to observe and be engaged; it is imperative to acknowledge their presence with enthusiasm.

In many small to mid-sized companies, the dilemma of staffing can often prevent taking advantage of these incredible marketing opportunities. Exhibiting at a trade show can certainly be turned into an effective experience if you have enough marketing materials and pertinent information for a potential client to read while they wait for you to complete a conversation with someone else.

If budget isn't an issue, an exhibit management company can effectively increase the return on your trade show investment by providing important logistical, administrative, staffing, research and management services. Their intimate understanding of the many issues unique to trade shows can be very beneficial.

Seven steps Toward a Successful Trade Show Experience

1. Ascertain which trade show(s) attracts your customers.

2. Start working on your budget.

3. Develop a marketing plan specific to your trade show audience, which includes a pre- and post-show public relations strategy.

4. Contact the convention bureau of the trade show's host city to identify local vendors.

5. Design your booth, collateral materials and appropriate specialty items with the same message and your full contact information.

6. Contact trade show management for demographic information, social events and show hours.

7. Develop a sales training workshop for employees or temporary staff.

You have made the decision to invest in an appropriate trade show, and your laser-focused planning is in place and is being executed. The training program is filled with powerful information, and the staff is excited. Your booth is professional, and your message is clear. Now, it is time to close the deals and watch your business grow.

MARSHA REEVES JEWS
The Bissell Street Group

Together we can make a difference:
focus, execution, results

(410) 300-6887
marsha@bissellstreet.com
www.bissellstreet.com

Marsha is a consummate entrepreneur and the founder of the Bissell Street Group, based in the Baltimore/Washington area with a national and Caribbean client base. Her clients reflect a broad spectrum of small and mid-sized businesses, NGOs, educational institutions and municipalities. Marsha's primary business competencies are marketing and business development.

A national leader in developing trade shows, conferences, seminars and career fairs, Marsha has worked with an array of Fortune 500 corporations as well as small and minority businesses, assisting with their trade show marketing strategies. Marsha's out-of-the-box thinking creates an environment of excitement on the exhibit hall floor and utilizes the most innovative marketing strategies for product exposure.

An avid reader and researcher, Marsha is committed to learning every aspect of her clients' businesses, their industries and competitors. Her creativity, enthusiasm and passion are infectious; her clients have a great time while accomplishing the mission.

Marsha has received numerous awards including the Mercedes Benz Vision Award for the founding of the Women of Color Technology Awards Conference. As a much sought-after public speaker, her dynamic and pithy style is unpredictable, entertaining and inspirational. With Marsha, you can always expect the unexpected!

And Now...The Big Payoff
Developing Your Exit Strategy
By Jennifer Howard

*I*n the fall of 2004, I handed the keys to my business, a lovely art gallery and custom frame shop on the Gulf Coast of Florida, over to a real estate attorney. The new owners of my now-former building lived out of the area; I never met them. All the money from the sale went to the bank; I never saw a dime.

Years later, when I took a good, long look at that business, I realized that it failed because I had not properly planned for its growth, but even more importantly, I had not planned for my exit. Do you have an exit strategy? Today, few small business owners I meet or work with have an exit strategy. I do not want what happened to me to happen to you.

What Is an Exit Strategy?

An exit strategy is a plan that is rarely discussed in a business plan, vision or even around the dinner table. The closest you will get to this type of planning is working with your life insurance agent on your "when-something-happens" plan. Often, your exit strategy determines whether you leave your business with lots of cash, little or no cash or owing money to someone else.

Why Do You Need an Exit Strategy?

When was the last time you sat down and wrote out what you wanted in life? Does the rest of your life involve never leaving your business? You may love and thoroughly enjoy what you are doing every day, but there should be more. For example, I know I want to spend many years enjoying my husband, children and grandchildren after exiting from the business. My exit plan involves travel, volunteering, church mission trips, having the time to tend a garden and much more. One of the reasons I began my business was to have the freedom to depart from it when and how I chose.

Your exit strategy should be one of the most important plans you put together for your business and for your life.

When you launched your business, did you consciously think of the day when you would exit it?

If you are like most people, you only thought of how excited you were because now you were on the path you had been dreaming about for years.

I want to share a secret with you that few small business owners know: your big financial payoff from owning and operating your business occurs when you sell it. Why? Because when you exit from your business and sell it to someone else, you receive your financial reward from all the years of "sweat equity," careful budgeting and surviving the ups and downs.

So, how do you get to the big payoff? You need an outstanding exit strategy that maximizes your business's value to potential buyers.

The Components of an Outstanding Exit Strategy

A very detailed and well-designed exit strategy could fill a three-inch or larger binder. You can also write a great plan in eight to ten pages. In your plan, the following components are vital:

• When you plan to exit

• The succession plan

• Key person insurance

• Fully documented business systems and processes

Additionally, you may choose to include:

• Current business valuation

• Up-to-date market analysis

• Key employee insurance

Let us look at each part of the exit strategy and its importance.

When You Plan to Exit

Most business owners plan to keep and work the business until retirement. A few will buy or begin a business with the intention of quickly building it into a successful entity and then selling it for a profit (flipping). A planned exit is important in both instances.

If you are working toward retirement, a plan to depart from your working life is, in essence, a plan to enjoy the fruits of your labor. Pinpointing the goal of the "exit time" opens the door to planning the years after you sell your business.

You may decide that your "exit date" goal is at a certain age or a particular calendar year. It does not matter. What does matter is making a decision and building your exit strategy from there.

The Succession Plan

Not every business owner readily knows who will take over the business. There are five different succession scenarios to consider:

- **Family member.** If you have a child or other member of your family who is interested in buying your business, exiting can be a simple process. Of course, working with family can have as many disadvantages as advantages, so you need to carefully consider this option. The one piece of advice I will offer is when family is involved, strongly consider having them buy the business instead of your handing it down. An entity that a person must purchase generally holds greater value than one that is given to them.

- **Business partner.** Your business partner, if you have one, is a natural consideration when selling your share of the company.

- **Key employee.** If you have hired well and employed career-minded people, a key employee could be a qualified prospect for your successor.

- **Competitor buyout.** Selling your business to a competitor is common. In your exit strategy, identify competitors who may be interested in owning your business.

- **Interested outsider.** Often, the interested outsider is a customer, vendor or friend. Writing down a few names that pop into your head is a great idea and can even be strategic.

In your succession plan, it is wise to include your intentions for assisting the new owner. If you are selling to a family member, you may stay involved for a time as a board member or advisor. When your buyer is a key employee or interested outsider, they may ask you to remain on as a consultant for a period of time. Business partners and competitors will usually not ask you for continued involvement. While it is not necessary to make this decision now, it will be a matter for consideration at the time of the sale.

With the exception of a family member, in most cases, you may be asked to sign a non-compete agreement. This type of contract states that you will not begin another business of the same type. Decide if this is a situation you can live with and for what period of time. Many non-compete agreements are three to five years in length; others may be through perpetuity. If you are exiting to retirement, a non-compete agreement will not be an important issue.

Finance Options

In your succession plan, it is wise to determine the financial options you are willing to consider. The top three are lease option, owner financing and, of course, cash.

- **Lease option** is similar to a rent-to-own plan for buying a home. The buyer has an opportunity to learn the business while you continue to actually own it.

- By providing **owner financing** to the buyer, you are generally able to remain close to your reasonable asking price. The downside is that if the buyer closes or exits the business before the end of your contract, you may end up in a legal situation to retrieve any balance the person owes you.

- **Cash** is certainly the most desirable way to be compensated for the sale of your business.

Key Person Insurance

Do you carry life insurance to assist your loved ones in the event of your death? What happens if you die or are severely disabled before you are able to carry out your exit plan? Unfortunately, your family may have to divert personal insurance funds or savings to cover the interruption of business, hiring and training a successor, preparing the business for sale or liquidating and closing the doors.

Investing in a separate insurance policy that would cover the business in the event of your death or disability is a smart and considerate action. The good news is that the business pays the premiums and is the actual beneficiary. Some financial institutions may require you to carry this type of insurance coverage as well, naming them as the beneficiary.

Your Guide to the Systems and Processes within the Business

Do you ever wonder why franchise businesses are so popular and so expensive? They are popular because the plan for operating it is already in place. They are expensive because someone else has spent years working out and perfecting that plan. You are paying for his or her time and hard work.

Beginning now, put together a binder that holds documentation of any system in your business. A system is a method you have developed or used to achieve something. This could include how you mix and how long you bake your famous cheesecake, or your special method and the materials you use for cleaning a commercial office. Your systems are your tried and true practices that set you apart from your competition.

Include in that binder a section that identifies your processes. A process is a series of specific actions that move something toward a result. If you have a sequence of how you move your customers through the sales procedure toward receiving the goods and lastly being surveyed on their level of customer satisfaction, this is your special process.

Everything you do in your business and how you do it should be written down and placed in your systems and process binder. When it is time to exit your business, you hand your binder to the buyer. If the documentation is carefully detailed and complete, the new owner should be able to continue running the business without missing a beat. In addition, your business instantly becomes more valuable because you have a blueprint for its successful operation. You have created a one-shop franchise!

Optional Components of Your Exit Strategy

- **Business valuation.** Do you know what your business is worth if you had to sell it today? Many CPAs are qualified to research and prepare a basic business valuation. A formal valuation is best left to a professional preparer and can cost thousands of dollars. However, a basic assessment is quite reasonable and is a great tool to evaluate areas of your business in which you would like to increase or add value.

- **Up-to-date market analysis.** A market analysis evaluates many factors, such as potential growth, market trends (local, national and possibly global) and a current profitability forecast. This tool can come in handy in a couple of different ways. First, it is a strategic planning method that assures your buyer you are an astute businessperson. By having this information updated each year, you are aware of the growth potential and possible decline of your type of business in the marketplace, as well as market trends overall. Second, it may also serve as a red flag or warning of potential market changes that could affect your business. If your exit strategy is in place, and you see a possible threat to your type of business, you might move up your exit date.

Let's say you own a family-run oil company in Oklahoma. Your up-to-date market analysis indicates that in five to seven years, oil drilling will become obsolete because of a new government regulation. You decide not to purchase the twenty drilling rigs you had planned to order this year. Instead, you contact the large national oil company that showed interest in your business a few months ago. You are moving up your exit from this business and think there is a future in wind energy. Alternatively, you are excited to take the money you receive and enjoy your retirement a little earlier.

• **Key person insurance on key employees.** When I put the art gallery up for sale, one valuable selling point was the framer I employed. In fact, her loyalty to the business was one of the reasons I had bought it five years earlier. In the middle of the selling process, my key employee had a heart attack and passed away a few months later. We were personally devastated at the loss, and her death moved us from being able to sell the business to liquidating it. I was moving to another state with my husband and would not be present to assist and provide training for a new owner. The framer had been the person who would have stayed with the business to fill this role. If I had key employee insurance on her, I could have hired and trained another framer. Additionally, I may have decided to drop the selling price and found a buyer because of the financial cushion the insurance money would have provided to the business.

The Exit

The vast majority of people who own their own small business will leave it when they choose. My wish for you is that your exit will be a happy occasion when you sell the business to someone else and walk away with your big payoff.

There is another way of exiting your business to which I referred earlier—severe disability or early death. I know this is an unpleasant subject, but as a business owner, you must factor these possibilities into your exit strategy.

Your family. In the key person insurance section, we discussed the insurance proceeds and the value they can provide for your family. It is important to identify what you would like your family to do with your business. If you are married, will your spouse take over the business or will he or she decide to sell it? Your succession plan should answer this question and provide detailed instructions in this event. If you are unmarried, your family (parents and siblings, usually) will bear the burden of deciding what to do with the company. Consider these factors and address them in your succession plan or your personal last will and testament.

The business partner. If you have a partner and do not have a buy-sell agreement in place, please see your legal advisor and implement one immediately. The buy-sell agreement spells out the answers to all the "what if's" that could take place in the event one of you leaves the business early or becomes disabled or dies. This agreement is especially important if one of you is not interested in remaining in business.

And Now, "The End"

If I had an exit strategy in place when I owned the art gallery I:

• Could have actually sold the business instead of having to close and liquidate it.

• Would have avoided a tremendous amount of stress and worry.

• Would have had a great financial base with which to begin a new business.

My advice to you: Do not make it complicated, do not stress over it, do not put it off. Do it. Build your exit strategy now, and it will pay many dividends later.

JENNIFER HOWARD
Small Business Coach
Next Level Group

Transform your business;
transform your life.

(405) 330-0611
jennifer@nextlevelgo.com
www.nextlevelgo.com

Possessing an intense desire to support entrepreneurial growth, Jennifer Howard launched Next Level Group, a small business coaching firm.

Next Level Group collaborates with the business owner to stabilize and grow a business that supports his or her life goals. Jennifer is an expert small business coach and her clients consider her a valuable partner in their growth and success. One client recently remarked, *"Jennifer 'gets' businesses and understands what it takes to make them grow and be successful. I am so thankful that I decided to get support, as I would never be to the point where I truly feel like I am running a business and not just working for one. My decision to hire Jennifer was the single best strategic business decision I could have ever made as a small business owner."*

A former corporate fix-it person, retail business owner and sales mentor for over twenty years, Jennifer is the past president of the South Central Chapter of Association of Image Consultants International, and a contributing member of the International Coach Federation. Additionally, she has numerous community affiliations, is a trained business coach, mentor and a certified image consultant.

More Incredible Business

Now that you have learned many things about how to build your business with a wide variety of tips, techniques and strategies, the next step is to take action. Get started applying what you have learned in the pages of this book.

We want you to know that we are here to help you meet your professional and personal objectives. The following pages list where we are geographically located. Regardless of where our companies are, many of us provide a variety of services over the phone or through webinars, and also welcome the opportunity to travel to your location or invite you to ours.

You can find out more about each of us by reading our bios at the end of our chapters, or by visiting our websites listed on the next pages. When you are ready for one-on-one consulting or group training or coaching from any of the co-authors in this book—we are available! Call us and let us know you have read our book, and we will provide you with a free phone consultation to determine your needs and how we can best serve you.

Alabama

Victoria Ashford   www.fearlessleading.com

Karen Sladick   www.organize4results.com

California

Karen Clark   www.mybusinesspresence.com

Sheri Cockrell   www.womensbusinessplanning.com

Pat Duran   www.awentrepreneur.com

Dezi Koster   www.dezikoster.com

Joanne Lang   www.thepersonalassistant.com

Tiffany Nielsen   www.tiffanynielsen.com

Caterina Rando, MA, MCC   www.attractclientswithease.com
                                    www.caterinaspeaks.com
                                    www.thrivebooks.com

Connecticut

Marge Piccini   www.margepiccini.com

Hawaii

Sylvia Dolena   www.awentrepreneur.com

Louisiana

Suzanne Zazulak Pedro, CPC   www.theprotocolpraxis.com

Maryland

Marsha Reeves Jews   www.bissellstreet.com

Missouri

Darlene Willman   www.accomplishmagazine.com
www.ussmallbusinessconference.com

Nevada

Kathy Carrico   www.kathycarrico.com

Oklahoma

Jennifer Howard   www.nextlevelgo.com

Pennsylvania

Mary Kot, AICI FLC   www.execimpressions.com

Texas

Mike Coy, RFC, CPBS   www.referraltrainingcenters.com
Sylvia A. Stern   www.re-imagebysylvia.com

Virginia

Vernice "FlyGirl" Armour, CCS   www.vernicearmour.com

Washington

Suzie Read   www.suzieread.com
Nancy LaMont   www.beeroyallyorganized.com

Thrive Publishing™ develops books for experts who want to share their knowledge with more and more people. We provide our co-authors with a proven system, professional guidance and support, producing quality, multi-author, how-to books that uplift and enhance the personal and professional lives of the people they serve.

We know that getting a book written and published is a huge undertaking. To make that process as easy as possible, we have an experienced team with the resources and know-how to put a quality, informative book in the hands of our co-authors quickly and affordably. Our co-authors are proud to be included in Thrive Publishing™ books because these publications enhance their business missions, give them a professional outreach tool and enable them to communicate essential information to a wider audience.

You can find out more about our upcoming book projects at
www.thrivebooks.com

Also from
Thrive Publishing™

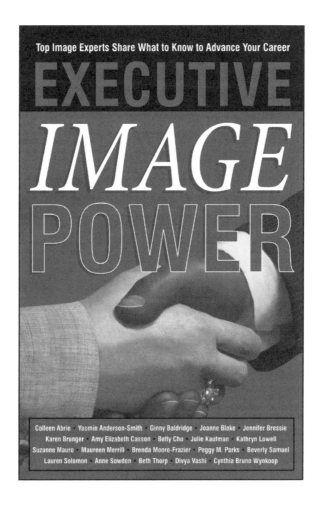

For more information on this book, visit
www.executiveimagebook.com

Also from
Thrive Publishing™

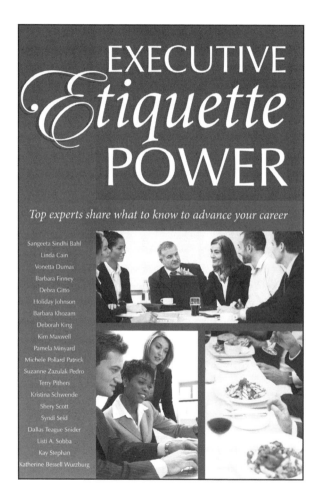

For more information on this book, visit
www.execetiquette.com

Also from
Thrive Publishing™

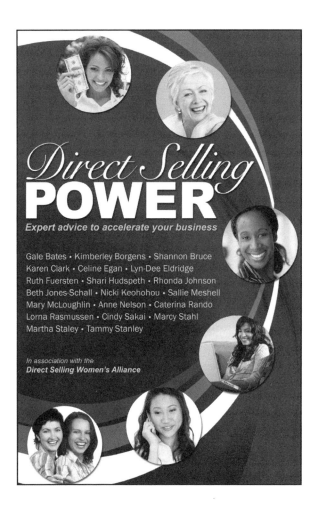

For more information on this book, visit
www.directsellingbook.com

Also from
Thrive Publishing™

TOP IMAGE EXPERTS
reveal strategies to always
look and be your best

INSPIRED
Style

Ginny Baldridge • Michele Bayle • Shirley Borrelli • Mari Bowlin
Chris Fulkerson • Pat Gray • Milena Joy • Barbara Layne • Carrie Leum
Julie Maeder • Lisa Ann Martin • Teresa McCarthy • Cynthia Lee Miller
Oreet Mizrahi • Sandy Moore • Cheryl Obermiller • Deborah Reynolds
Sally Templeton • Dominique Vaughan-Russell • Alison Vaughn • Debbie Wright

For more information on this book, visit
www.inspiredstylebook.com

**Also from
Thrive Publishing™**

**Get
Organized
TODAY**

Top experts share strategies that work

Toni Ahlgren · Anne Blumer
Nancy Castelli · Gretchen Ditto · Rhonda Elliott
Bibi Goldstein · Katie Munoz · Mary L. Noble
Tina Oscar · Natasha Packer · Scott Roewer
Janet Schiesl · JoAnn Scordino · Anna Sicalides
Melissa Stacey · Charlotte Steill · Sandy Stelter
Angela F. Wallace · Annette Watz

For more information on this book, visit
www.getorganizedtodaybook.com